Letters from The Way

A story of self-discovery on the Camino

ANGELA BARNARD

ISBN-13: 978-1986121224

For those yet to discover The Way may you find what you're looking for, or may it find you…

… it's already there within you, sometimes you just have to walk it out.

CONTENTS

Acknowledgements   vi

Preface: Forward looking back   1

A letter before the journey begins   4

A private journal entry before departure   6

Part I Letters from the Way

The first letter from Navarrete, Spain   11

The second letter from Villalcázar de Sirga, Spain   18

The third letter from Astorga, Spain   25

The fourth letter from Barbadelo, Spain   29

The fifth letter from Negreira, Spain   36

The sixth letter from Finisterre, Spain   42

The seventh letter from Angers, France   48

A brief interlude

A journal entry four days after returning   54

A few thoughts   58

A letter from my Camino first love   66

A journal entry on the day of departure   74

This was 'The End'   75

Part II Lessons from The Way

Blog post 1: The only way out is in   77

Blog post 2: Six resilience tips I learnt climbing the Pyrenees   82

Blog post 3: How walking the Camino taught me not to suffer   88

Blog post 4: Six simple actions to gain clarity   93

Blog post 5: What walking the Camino taught me about gratitude   97

Blog post 6: Three quick tips for remaining focused   101

Part III Back to The Way

The in-between story   106

The eighth letter from San Antón, Spain   113

The ninth letter from San Antón, Spain   118

The tenth letter from San Antón, Spain   122

The eleventh letter from San Antón, Spain   127

The twelfth letter from San Antón, Spain   132

The thirteenth letter from San Antón, Spain   136

The fourteenth letter from somewhere on the German Autobahn   141

Part IV After The Way

The fifteenth letter, which I never sent   153

The sixteenth letter from Holzminden, Germany   164

The seventeenth letter from Holzminden, Germany   176

About the author   185

ACKNOWLEDGEMENTS

We do not walk through this life in a vacuum, and I would like to thank all of those many people who have contributed to my growth and development in my life. I thank you all for the roles you have played, both positively and negatively. In this thing called life, everything contributes to the whole.

To my family, passed and living, thank you for your love and encouragement and for teaching me the skills I needed to walk this journey of life. I love you all.

To my Camino family, thank you for walking into my life. I carry you all in my heart. Brendan, thank you for getting me over the Pyrenees and allowing me to share your story in this book.

To my editor extraordinaire, Liz Hudson from Little Red Pen, thank you!

To the team at Design for Writers for the beautiful cover, thank you!

Diana thank you for helping me reach my highest potential and believing in me to achieve anything I set my mind to. I love you!

'A journey of a thousand miles begins with a single step.' – Lao-Tzu

Preface

Forward Looking Back

How often in life are we not clueless? With the advantage of hindsight, we can examine the picture and see something very different, or we can finally see how the dots join.

For many years, my friends Robert and Jeannette would join Diana, my partner (lovingly known as 'The German'), and I for dinner. Late into the night, we would discuss life in general, touching upon favourite topics, one of them being exercise. Essentially, I am lazy and don't particularly enjoy exercising. Diana and our friends love it. Jeannette often encouraged me to consider Nordic walking, and I would listen politely but never follow up.

In 2012, I started a new job, which I loved, and moved away from our home base of Holzminden, in Germany. The German and I began a gruelling long-distance relationship and spent weekends travelling to see one another. In between excessive business travel I tried to settle into my new hometown of Brühl, meet new people and develop different hobbies. I saw a course advertised at the local community centre, Nordic Walking: An Introduction, and, as it took place at the weekend, I signed Diana and myself up so we could investigate the sport.

Surprisingly, I loved it! I quickly got the hang of how to walk, and the following week I went to a local sports store and kitted myself out with sticks, shoes and socks. I mentioned to a colleague what I was doing. She too loved walking, so we started a weekly ritual where after work we would walk around the lakes near her home. Close to both of my residences were beautiful forests, lakes and rivers, and The German and I would enjoy the outdoors at least once a weekend. I had upped my movement from 0 kilometres to approximately 10 kilometres per week – a radical improvement. However, I was no more in love with exercising than before.

Is it possible that these simple events, all strung together over a period of years, were preparing me for what was to come?

That job I loved nearly killed me. It might sound dramatic, but it's the truth. While I loved what I was creating with the team, my narcissistic Machiavellian boss did not and began a process of workplace bullying against me. I fell into crisis, became ill, and there were moments when I felt I had reached the end of my tether. I was shocked and horrified by this. How was it possible for me to descend to such levels of despair?

This unfolding story begins shortly after emerging from this crisis and despair. This is not a tale of woe and suffering but rather one of resilience and persistence in my 'mad' quest to follow my heart and discover what was waiting for me on the other side of a million steps. I hope my story will challenge and inspire you.

A Letter before the Journey Begins

From: Angela Barnard, making_hay@yahoo.co.uk
To: Dear Friends
Subject: The Way of Saint James/Camino de Santiago/
Der Jakobsweg
Date: Friday, 13 June 2014, 10:20

Darlings

As some of you know, I have endured deeply traumatic workplace bullying since November last year, and my life has undergone some relatively radical changes in the last months. After accepting a settlement package from that company I have time on my hands to consider the meaning of life and, more specifically, what I want from this life.

This journey has led me to the conclusion that I need to go walkabout, so this coming Monday I am leaving Germany and heading off to France to walk to Santiago de Compostela. Since April, I have had an overwhelming urge to simply pack a bag and walk. As I was leaving my niece in Canada on 20th May, I spontaneously said to her, 'Bianca I think I'm going to walk the Camino.' A week later in the Italian Alps I finalised that decision, and, well, here we go …

I expect to start walking the Camino Francés, one of the Camino routes through Spain, next Wednesday and am extremely hopeful that I will complete the journey, all 789 designated kilometres. I hope that I will be able to finish sometime around my birthday if all goes well.

As someone who never deliberates over the trip I am about to embark on, I find my sense of expectancy and excitement extremely high for this journey. Perhaps it is madness.

I will be leaving The German, my phone and most worldly possessions in Germany and am praying that I meet angels and friends and experience all that I need to on The Way.

Your positive thoughts, prayers and well wishes would all be most appreciated. If I pop into your mind, please send up a thought or prayer on my behalf as at that exact moment I may need it.

I am hoping that my body remains healthy, my mind is focused and clear and my spirit is cognisant of all it needs to hear and receive. Most of all, I am hoping that I can be brave and see this through, and, oh dear God, that I will float like a butterfly over the Pyrenees.

Best wishes,

Angie

A Private Journal Entry before Departure

Sunday, 15 June 2014, 08:42

Today is my last day before I leave on the Camino. I am feeling slightly overwhelmed by the prospect of it all, but I am also feeling expectant and excited.

'Is what we are looking for the same as what we will find?' This is a quote by Mark Shea from his documentary, *The Way: One Man's Spiritual Journey along the Camino de Santiago*. It's a very moving and eloquent account of his journey in 2004. I find this question quite powerful because many times they are not the same thing. Mostly what we find is so much more enriching than what we thought we were seeking.

I am looking for a lot on this journey. Mostly I am looking for acceptance of my true self. I am also looking for a way, a spark or a kick up the ass that I will start following my dreams and overcome my fears. I mean, what exactly is fear? Is it a thought? A belief (which is a thought practised many times)? An action? An experience? A hormonal reaction? An emotion? A learnt behaviour?

For myself, the most fearless place I can be is in this moment. When I am overwhelmed and slide into fear,

I need to stop, take a moment, regulate my breath and simply evaluate this moment. How am I? Is all well with my soul? Is anything harming me? Fearing the past or events which have occurred and which could perhaps reoccur is actually living in the past. It's like a dog eating its own vomit. Why would I want to do that?

Being present in the now and fearing imaginary events is also madness. Fearing scenarios that might occur based on experience or future projection is utter madness. How can I waste my time of now fearing something which has not yet happened and which is unlikely to occur? The 'what ifs' are actually self-induced madness! When I start to fear the future, I can follow the rabbit down its burrow, or I can choose another way.

Overcoming fear is simply a choice … especially when there is no imminent bodily danger present. I look around me and consider how much fear we manufacture each day: in our speech, in the TV we watch, in the books we read, in the news we hear, in the emotions we feel. The world is constantly manufacturing fear, spewing it forth, it's growing, festering, spreading … how do I fit into this cycle? How do I add to the disease? I know that I do this, and, as of today, I consciously commit to stop being a part of the problem.

What do I fear about the Camino?

That I won't finish. This is not true. I will!

That my shoes are not the right ones. This is not true. They are very comfortable and protect my feet well.

That the pathway will be too difficult to navigate in my shoes. I just need to tread lightly and be aware and concentrated.

That I won't find shelter for the night. This is not true. I will always find a place to sleep.

That I will lose my way. This is not true. At every moment along The Way, I will be in just the right place, and there are *always* angels to guide me.

That the weather will be extreme and will make The Way difficult. The weather will be as it is, and I will cope with the situation.

That someone will try to do me harm. I have never been harmed in my life, why would it start now? And am I not totally protected by my angels and guides?

There is nothing to fear! Even now, as I sit here, I ask Spirit to help me remain focused and clear-headed. When I am overwhelmed by fear, may I be reminded of these lessons which I have learnt. Banish fear. Move beyond fear's stagnation. Listen to your heart! Are fears true? Can they happen? Will they harm or kill me? NO, YES, NO. Sometimes you have to be scared to step out and do it anyway. A journey always begins with the first step. Even a journey to overcome my fears begins with the first step. I just need to take it.

So on the last morning before I leave the safety and security of my own home, I give thanks for each moment that is and each moment that is to come. Thank you for bringing me to this point where I am aware of following The Way. Thank you for the good things that are happening in my heart, soul and mind. Thank you for my angels and guides who are with me always, willing to help me.

PART I

LETTERS FROM THE WAY

'The reason we are walking this way is to overcome our limits. If only we could overcome our limits, then we would see how endless our potential is.' – Jürg Ellenberger

The First Letter from Navarrete, Spain

From: Angela Barnard, making_hay@yahoo.co.uk
To: Dear Friends
Subject: Buddha is wrong!
Date: Wednesday, 25 June 2014, 13:07

According to Buddha, attachment to things causes suffering … Well, I can say with 100-per-cent certainty, darling Buddha is WRONG! Walking the friggin' Camino causes suffering! I have tried to lose my attachment to the backpack; it does not want to leave. The feet refuse to head off and service another masochist, and the friggin' head keeps repeating, with drum-like precision after every step: 'Thank! You! Thank! You! Thank! You!' How do I lose the attachment, thereby releasing myself from suffering? Moreover, not just suffering, but suffering over my suffering!

I have blisters on my feet, parts of which I never knew existed, and blisters on my lips. My head feels like a gigantic blister from boiling in its own foul juices under a sweat-drenched hat. In fact, my blisters now have blisters. I have shin splints. I have suffered from twenty-four-hour diarrhoea. These hips will most definitely never be child-bearing, and I am being eaten alive by every friggin' bug in Spain …

Yet I am having an abso-bladdy marvellous friggin' time!

My journey began on Monday, 16 June. I was supposed to travel by train, but the dear French decided to strike, and I changed plans and drove myself 1,829.2 kilometres, taking nineteen hours and fourteen minutes to reach Saint-Jean-Pied-de-Port in France. The drive was peaceful and uneventful, and my iPod played spectacular music the whole way. Many times I was singing so loud I could just vomit from exertion.

On Wednesday morning, bright and early, I hit the track, heading over the Pyrenees towards Spain. Oh dear God in Heaven, what was I thinking? The first 8 kilometres after leaving Saint-Jean-Pied-de-Port felt like a sheer vertical climb up a rock face. This did not improve for the next 13 kilometres, although it did ease off slightly. Within the first 10 kilometres, I was more than ready to stick out my thumb and hitch a ride but upwards and onwards I trudged. Thank God I organised transportation for the backpack that first day; otherwise, I think I would not have made it.

Before leaving for this trip, I had a reiki appointment that I felt I had to keep. After a stunning session with the practitioner Burgunde Thorn, and as I was leaving her practice, she told me to pay special attention to people's stories. This confirmed what my heart had been telling me.

The first story I encountered was on the German Autobahn. People do not stop on the Autobahn to make friends. They race along like lunatics, tear into a rest stop, run to the toilet, elbowing old grannies from tour buses out the way, grab a bite, or drink quick! quick! then tear off down the track again. They do not dilly-dally. I stopped to relieve myself and pulled up next to a car from Ireland. I thought, *How unusual, such a rare sight*. Even as I disembarked, the woman from the vehicle was already in full conversation with me. Taken by surprise, I stopped to listen to her telling me of her grand tour to the south with her canary (happily ensconced in the back) and her grumpy-looking hubby. I acknowledged her, wanting to move on, and she gave me a super-fast rundown of her life. At first I wondered if this was speed dating on the Autobahn. Later, as I sat on the loo, I burst out laughing. I knew I had to take the time to listen to people's stories.

So there I was, going up the sheer cliff face, or so it seemed, 10 kilometres behind me and another friggin' 779 kilometres to go. I stopped and said, 'Dear God, I really need help. I don't think I can do this.'

Earlier, I had been sitting on a rock, and a man came around the corner looking shattered. I offered him a seat next to me. He grunted something unintelligible, and I was not sure what his mother tongue was. Later, after breaking at an *albergue* (hostel), he passed me, and I could see him suffering ahead of me.

Trudge! Trudge! Trudge!

I rounded a bend, and there he was, sitting on a rock taking pictures and singing along to 'Angie' by The Rolling Stones. I chatted to him briefly, introduced myself and asked if he wanted to suffer together. He told me he would love to, so Brendan and I walked the next 14 kilometres together. Two days later, Brendan said to me that he felt he had sung me up the mountain to him so that we could conquer it together, and I thought that was so true.

In between heaving breaths, we discussed the basics about ourselves. I phrased my question regarding his purpose for doing the Camino in a rather irreverent, flippant manner. A stillness came over him, and I felt emotion pouring off him. He then told me something so personal and intimate that I stood on the mountain with him and just cried. He was also crying, his pain and suffering so deep, and saying, 'I don't know why I'm telling you this, I barely know you.' I was so moved and honoured to hear his story. I asked if I could touch him and laid my hands on his heart and his head and asked for healing and restoration to occur for him during this walk.

Since meeting Brendan, I have encountered amazing people with incredible stories. Ines, the German mother of two (a four-year-old son and two-year-old daughter), dragging a stroller up and down the mountains. Jurien from northern Holland, who walked out of his front door ten weeks ago and started his pilgrimage. Tom, a sixty-nine-year-old Scot who felt the hand of God raise him from his deathbed of alcoholism and drugs forty years ago and tell him that He would change his life and for him to walk the Camino. It's taken him forty years. Roy and Sylvia, the most wonderful couple from Los Angeles, who have such an amazing love, respect and relationship to each other. Dear sweet Yeong Ju from South Korea who told me he is the most boring person he knows and that he has no precious memories in his life so he is walking the Camino to acquire some precious memories. My heart really went out to him, and I told him that I was sure this would be a walk filled with many memories. He replied, saying, 'Ah, but of course, Ann Jie. You are now one of my precious memories.' There was Jürg, the Swiss man I met in an *albergue* in Zubiri, who said something so profound and wise to me that I became extremely emotional as I absorbed his message. I told him how deeply moved I was, and we then held hands and cried together for a moment. I may likely never see him again, but I have that small gem that I will take with me for ever.

Then, of course, the dark side ... Walking through a beautiful forest, we encountered Pablo the singing artist, who likes to entertain the walking masses and sell them photos of his supposed art. I found nothing remotely interesting about this man, and I just wanted to get away from him ASAP. At the next stop, pilgrims were discussing their day, and Juan, a fellow pilgrim, asked if any of us had encountered Pablo. He went on to tell us that when he had sat and chatted with him, Pablo had spewed so much hatred for the world, specifically gay and lesbian people. Sylvia looked at me as if I had just landed from Mars. She said it had been bothering her how my body language had changed so dramatically when I came near Pablo. If the guy had not been 3.5 kilometres away, I would have returned and bitch-slapped him ten ways sideways and perhaps given him a legitimate reason to hate lesbians.

Then there was Ronald from Santa Fe. He gave me the heebie-jeebies. I chatted to him briefly and found that he exuded a strange energy. I just did not want to engage with him. He told me I reminded him of someone he used to work with. I felt that I should not dig deeper, but two days later, in front of a group of people, he again told me that I reminded him of someone. He went on to say that he found my image elicited strong feelings of negativity in him erupting from this past relationship. He asked if I found his image bringing things to the fore for me, that I needed to work on. Honest to God, I had to hold myself back. I politely told him that he was on his own in that respect and that I would try to keep my image away from offending him, but good luck with working through past issues. Good God, does the man really want to carry me as a burden the rest of the way?

The daily trudge continues. My pain and suffering continue. The pilgrims I travel with come and go. Every day, the new sights and sounds seem to explode before my eyes. I am travelling at a snail's pace, but I feel I have imbibed so much – enough for a lifetime. Only a week has passed, and yet it feels so much longer. Thanks to so many of you who sent me words of encouragement and blessings before I left. Your voices and words have popped into my mind at opportune moments, and I thank you all for the encouragement …

Continue to light bonfires of candles: I need them! It is time to go off and find the Camino.

Lots of love and blessings from Navarrete,

Angie

The Second Letter from Villalcázar De Sirga, Spain

From: Angela Barnard, making_hay@yahoo.co.uk
To: Dear Friends
Subject: Crying hot tears over ice and black tea
Date: Saturday, 5 July 2014, 15:25

I have been on this journey eighteen days: seventeen walking and one rest day, 369 kilometres trudged along, and 420 kilometres still to go ...

I left the gorgeous fairy-tale city of Burgos on Wednesday morning at 6:30 a.m. to the sight and sound of drunken revellers returning to their nests after a night of partying and drinking. This seems to be quite normal in Spain. The people keep going until 7 a.m., stumble wherever and continue later. It is currently the festival of Saint Peter and Saint Paul, meaning two weeks of drunken madness, various cultural activities, live street performances and gorgeous food. I seriously had to forgive an American pilgrim who gasped when they first saw the city gate and cathedral of Burgos, exclaiming, 'Oh, wow, we

only see things like this in Vegas and Disney World!'
As a city, it really is a marvel, and the cathedral is just
mind-blowing.

After the rest day in Burgos – big city life and
enjoying some alone time in a hotel, total decadence –
we got back on the road again, heading off into the
Meseta. These are the flat plains of Spain, consisting of
nothing but wheat and barley fields. Apparently they
are the site of mental breakdowns amongst pilgrims:
attempted strangulation with wheat stalks, drowning in
rain puddles. Due to the rest day, I lost some of the
family of pilgrims I was travelling with and am now
encountering new odd-bods. It is actually amazing
how many gaga-lagas are trying to complete this
pilgrimage in twenty days or less. I rather wonder what
is the point, but each to their own. Leaving Burgos
was a revelation once again of my character and the
character of my fellow travellers. I had the feeling,
after a day off in a beautiful city, of wanting to settle,
to stay a while and forget The Way. This made me
realise again how seductive distractions can be and
how quickly I can settle for things that I know are
second-best. So I pulled myself together and headed
for the Meseta and apparent certain death.

My health issues have not improved. My blisters
have become grandparents. The shins have tendinitis.
The head blisters are slowly healing. The back is
aching. There are shooting pains running up the legs.
Toenails have fallen off … And blah, blah, blah. None

of this is unique to me. Many have been hospitalised or have been forced to stop by doctors. In the general scheme of things, I am doing well. One just kind of walks through the pain and, with drum-like precision, gives thanks to whichever gods are keeping one upright at that given moment.

Burgos to Hornillos del Camino was no different. The shins were screaming in agony, and the drugs were not working. Somewhere along the way, Roy gave me additional prescription medication for the pain, and, after a while, I could feel the effect on my empty stomach. Luckily, I had a bread roll in my bag and stomped along chewing cardboard with goat's cheese and old tomatoes.

Thank God that in my misery of pain I did not find the Meseta to be a place where I could end it all. In fact, I found just the opposite. The beauty of the landscape was awe-inspiring, and it was like walking through a Van Gogh masterpiece. The joy of walking in a halo of birdsong, watching the kaleidoscope emerald and gold movement of the barley and hearing the old women's voices of the wheat whispering *sh-sh-sh-sh-sh-sh* was wonderful. At various moments, the sky told diverse dramatic stories, and the simple wildflowers added colours and dimensions that were hard to fathom. I did not felt the need to strangle or drown myself, but trading in my shins for new ones became an obsession.

As we reached Cuesta de Matamulos (the Mule Killer Slope) that overlooks Hornillos, I finally felt the benefit of the goat's cheese and cardboard reach my stomach. I thought I was hallucinating as I watched the village shimmering in the distance and slowly made my way down the slope of doom and destruction. Coming onto the flat, I was transformed into a hamster on a wheel. My porky little legs started moving at super-speed, and my arms were rhythmically pumping along. Somewhere in the base of my skull I heard the voice of reason demanding that I slow down, but my mind was screaming in pain and my legs just kept spinning.

I overtook three other pilgrims who were walking quite fast, and in no time at all was in front of the village store. I went inside and ordered a cold Coke. The owner engaged me in conversation. I understood that he was asking if I was staying or moving on another 5 kilometres to the next stop. I showed him my shins and indicated that I was in pain and that it was impossible to continue. He yelled '*Infección!*', raised his hands in a stop signal and disappeared into the back.

He came back out with a frozen bottle of water and yelled 'like glass!' while smashing the bottle down on the counter. I thought, 'Oh God! First day in the Meseta and I'm gonna be killed by flying ice!' He told me to put the bottle on my shins, and I grabbed him, kissing him profusely with many 'Muchas gracias señor!' I sat in front of the store nursing myself, and eventually the rest of the group came along. When I entered the store to pay for the water, I received a profuse 'NO! NO!' from the owner. He took the bottle from my hand and disappeared into the back, returning with a larger bottle of frozen water. He then started hugging and kissing me profusely, wishing me 'Buen Camino!' I walked outside and promptly burst out crying. It was such a small little thing – an iced bottle of frozen water – but I was having a hot ugly cry over his simple caring and the Universe's ability to give me just what I needed in that moment.

For a few days I had been longing for a lovely cup of sweet black tea, like The German normally makes me after dinner. (This is coffee country, so tea is not commonly ordered.) On Thursday, we were trudging along and came to San Antón where the gorgeous ruins of the Convento de San Antón straddle the road. We thought there was a town nearby but could not see it in the distance so I suggested that we walk around the ruins to see if a town could be seen behind them. The only thing we saw was an *albergue* built into the beautiful relic.

I approached the entrance to see a man and woman eating lunch and asked if there was somewhere to buy food or drinks. The woman explained to me that it was an *albergue* and that they did not have those facilities. I asked to use the toilet, and she opened it for me to use. We took a moment to sit at a bench and soak up the tremendous atmosphere of this place, originally built in the 1100s. Then the woman approached me and asked if I would like a cup of tea. I was blown away and asked if it would be possible to have milk with it. She affirmed this and left to prepare the tea. I was so happy to see black tea amongst the varieties set on a simple tray with three clay cups, milk and gorgeous brown sugar and immediately made myself a cup. I cannot begin to express how good it tasted.

In Spanish, the woman told us the history of the place, a healing centre established by the San Antón Order who were able to heal people suffering from ergotism, or St Anthony's Fire, a fungal disease caused by eating infected barley bread. They administered herbal wine, pure white wheat bread and love, and apparently this healed people, who came from as far afield as Switzerland and Holland.

The woman's male companion tried to communicate in Spanish, and I wondered if he had a problem because it was so bad. When he came to clear the table, I thanked him in English, and he asked me where I was from. I told him, and learnt that he was an Irish priest. He asked me if I loved black tea, and I said, 'Yes I do, sweet, strong and with milk.' He went inside and returned with five teabags of strong Irish tea – apparently, one bag is strong enough for six cups. He pressed them into my hands, blessed me, and wished me great enjoyment drinking the tea and sharing it with others.

I was moved to tears, having to prevent myself from dissolving into ugly-cry mode again. As we left, the woman took my sweaty, grubby face in her tender hands, kissed me and embraced me with such love and compassion. She then did the same for my travelling companions. We were overcome with a sense of love and caring. To all three of us she smelt gorgeous! That was such a small gesture, such a tiny moment in eternity, that touched us to the core of our beings.

This is what the Camino is like: unexpected encounters of love and compassion from passing strangers or fellow travellers. Travelling at a snail's pace, it seems impossible not to receive unsolicited acts of love and kindness. Each day I look for them, and each day I try to offer them in return …

Love and blessings from Villalcázar de Sirga,

Angie

The Third Letter from Astorga, Spain

From: Angela Barnard, making_hay@yahoo.co.uk
To: Dear Friends
Subject: Needing solitude and feeling unsettled
Date: Thursday, 10 July 2014, 22:38

Well, I am now into my fourth week, with only eleven more days to go until I reach Santiago. I have passed the 500-kilometre mark, and it seems I might get there on my birthday. Wouldn't that be different? Nevertheless, let us wait and see as anything can still happen. We are about to go into the mountains again, and in about three days' time we should pass the highest point of the Camino. Then I can get rid of the rocks I have been carrying all this way!

Every day continues to be so simple and yet so different. I awake, dress, brush my teeth, hit the road, walk until breakfast, eat, walk until lunch, and eat. I take breaks, drink loads of water, pay attention to everything, observe the stillness of my mind, speak to people as I go, and reach my destination. I find a place to sleep, shower, do laundry, rest, tend to my feet, find dinner, eat, and find a Catholic Church to spy on their array of priceless treasures during Mass, meditate, keep my diary, and sleep.

As I listen to people along The Way, the message keeps coming through loud and clear. People ask themselves, 'What the hell am I doing with my life every day?' There are so many people like myself who are in transition, many business owners, teachers, parents with their kids, every type of person. We are struck by the absolute simplicity of The Way and how we carry so many unnecessary burdens in daily life.

On Monday, I was asking myself what I would do if I was required to give up 'everything' and how could I learn to practise more grace each day. I was faced with these realities sooner rather than later. A taxi driver took me for a joy ride and charged me more than agreed; additionally, he stopped the cab to pick up a hitchhiker who happened to be stoned. The smell of weed on him was so strong I wanted to gag. Faced with the dilemma of refusing the man a ride on my euro or being gracious in the Camino spirit and allowing the driver to help him, I chose the latter, blocking my nostrils so as not to vomit on him. I did get a peace sign and a garbled 'Buen Camino' from the stoned one.

On the same day, my backpack went missing. The only things in the bag were a second set of clothes, toiletries, an iPad, jacket and sandals , yet I felt panicked by the thought of 'losing everything'. Struck with a sense of loss, I noted how my brain immediately started imagining the worst-case scenario of having to return home. I realised that even if I didn't find the backpack, I would continue walking. This was a very valuable lesson for me, as it was applicable not only in the moment but to all aspects of my life. I was quite helpless, without language skills, familiar friends, phone, or contact numbers, but at exactly the moment when I needed her most, a multilingual angel came along who helped me find my bag.

As I stood at the roadside, a car passed me, and the driver made eye contact with me. She stopped and asked me with an American accent, 'Do you by any chance know Allison?' 'Do you mean Allison from Boston?' I asked. The woman was flabbergasted that I knew exactly whom she was speaking of, and I mentioned that I met Allison two nights prior in the middle of the Meseta where we shared a meal, and that the last time I saw her was the day before as she drove away in a cab, in a rather emotional state. I had Allison on my mind most of the day, hoping that she was OK, and the lady told me she had met Allison in a restaurant the night before with another pilgrim. She told me that she lived in a nearby town and the pilgrims walk directly past her house. She hoped to see Allison and her companion pass her house as she makes soaps and wanted to gift them some of her product. I mentioned that I had not seen either pilgrim but that I would take the soaps and pass them on when I encountered them again. It was a few days later that I bumped into them both in León and we were all amazed at the serendipity of the situation.

After handing over the soap, she asked if I was OK because I seemed rather distressed. I explained what had happened with my bag, that I could not remember the transportation company I used, the name of the town I last stayed in or the name of the *albergue*. With a few probing questions she managed to extract some information out of me and started working the phone to track down my bag. In fluent and loud Spanish she spoke to a few people and in no time discovered that the transportation company had made an error with my bag and were in the process of trying to get it to me. As we stood at the roadside, we saw a taxi they had hired to deliver my bag to me drive into town, thereby solving my problem and alleviating my anxiety.

As I start this fourth week, I am feeling a strong need to be solitary. I am also feeling shocked by how little time I have left and 'scared' that I will not figure out the purpose for being on this path. I know in my waters that I should not be scared and that I should continue, as I do every day, to be 'open' and alert, but I feel 'life looming', and this brings with it a sense of dread. Please send up prayers and thoughts for me because I feel I need it. Once again, thanks for all the love and well wishes.

Love and blessings from Astorga,
Angie

The Fourth Letter from Barbadelo, Spain

From: Angela Barnard, making_hay@yahoo.co.uk
To: Dear Friends
Subject: Losing my teeth and the sparrows of the fields
Date: Thursday, 17 July 2014, 21:01

The last update I sent was not a happy, peppy update with anecdotes of a pilgrim's suffering. I almost never sent that mail. However, I knew that because I am walking in truth I need to *tell* the truth about this experience.

I was so blessed by the encouragement I received. In fact, different people wrote to me with different responses, and I received wisdom not only from The Way but also from those who love me 'at home'. I felt pressure and had a sense that I was doing something 'wrong'. I listened to people speak about how they had been reflecting on their lives, working through things from the past, and I thought, *Oh fuck! I am not doing that!* In fact, I have spent the past five weeks present in the now. I almost have not thought about anything that has not been directly in my face or experience.

Two emails came through that really affected me. One was from my beloved niece, Bianca, who wrote, 'Have you ever thought that the purpose for being on this walk was to just be? Just meet people, travel by foot? Get out of the rut you may have been in? Maybe we don't need to seek purpose … Sometimes I think we need to just go with the flow and enjoy the privilege of being able to walk and see the world. Just food for thought!' That to me was a confirmation that everything was OK. There have been numerous days when I have plodded along singing 'Let It Be' by The Beatles and I have been struck by the awesome privilege of this experience.

The other mail suggested that I simply create space and leave everything else on The Way, that I don't go looking to acquire stuff but rather leave stuff behind and create space within myself. This is just what I needed to hear. It was pragmatic and expressed in a way that I could comprehend and then implement. I had been trying to do that but not as specifically as suggested, and it was the key I needed.

The next day, we were climbing up to Cruz de Ferro (the Iron Cross), situated on the highest point of the Camino Francés. The Iron Cross is a simple structure atop a long pole, a six-kilometre hike from the nearest town. People follow a tradition of leaving stones behind at the base, symbolic of burdens or hopes they might be carrying, and, over the years, the pile has risen quite high. For those of us who slept over in

Rabanal del Camino, the tension and excitement were quite palpable. Each person seemed to have their own expectations and hopes regarding the day. I just hoped to get up there in one piece.

Additionally, I was processing the advice I had received from a dream. That night, I had a terrible dream about three of my front teeth falling out. I looked for them desperately, finding them happily ensconced on my tongue, further back in my mouth. I was horrified by this dream and quite annoyed that I should have it the night before the 'big day'. Before I set off in the morning, I searched possible dream interpretations online. They were all quite relevant to my life at that moment, spoke of signs of personal expansion, and invited me to look at loss and personal growth. Teeth are symbols of strength and self-esteem, and losing one's teeth symbolises rebirth and reflects the tension and sometimes painful process that comes with starting or creating something new. The initial distress that I had about my front teeth going AWOL evolved into a mild form of hope that the Universe was trying to tell me something.

On Tuesday last week I was walking along the path from Religios to Mansilla de las Mulas as the sun was rising. It was a narrow gravel path with a grass verge in the middle. Suddenly, on the other side, I noticed something, and when I looked closely I saw it was a little sparrow. As some of you know, I love sparrows most of all the birds. I find their cheeky character, tenacity and the fact that they do not crap on everything greatly appealing. I walked with the little bird a while and noticed that for each step I was taking she was hopping along. It seemed like she wanted to fly but for some reason was unable to. I was not sure if she was too young or if she was injured. I felt a real connection to that little bird especially as she seemed to be accompanying me. I slowed to the point where I was just about to pick her up and take her back down the track to where we had met.

At that moment, two people came crashing up the path, the connection was broken, and the little bird became overwhelmed with fear and went into the bush. After they had crashed on by, she emerged and hopped back in the direction she came from. This encounter stayed with me for days. I believe that animals are sent to us with different messages, and I investigated sparrow medicine, which teaches of self-worth. If a sparrow is sent to you, you are encouraged to look at your self-worth and to build it. This really meant a lot to me because this has been a big issue that I have been dealing with, especially with the changes I want to make in my life.

So on Saturday morning I had a lot on my mind as I was climbing the mountain to Cruz de Ferro. I was thinking about how I could create space. Suddenly I was confronted with many thoughts and felt swamped with emotion. When I came upon the Cross, there were only six of us present and we had the moment to ourselves. The Cross was not what I expected, but in the greater scheme of things that was meaningless.

Before I left Germany, I picked up three stones, and I had been carrying them with me. I did not have a clear idea what the three stones symbolised, but, as I stepped onto the mound, it came to me, and, as I laid these burdens down, I was crying excessively. I had a clear sense that I should not be fearful of the future but that all would be well. I continued to cry as I came down the mound and sat quietly alone for a while.

As I was sitting alone, Patrick, a fellow pilgrim, came over and asked if I would like to join a Mass which a Spanish priest was offering at the picnic tables on the opposite side of the road. The priest, Padre Pablo, seemed to know Isabel and Maria, two Spanish women I had met two nights before. I asked what their association was and learned that he was their priest from Madrid. He had come all this way as a surprise to walk this stretch of the journey with them and to serve them communion at Cruz de Ferro. I felt moved by his actions.

Padre Pablo was a burly young man, exuding love, confidence and compassion – a truly lovely person. Everyone assisted in dressing the picnic table as an altar, with serviettes, stones, and various religious paraphernalia. Pablo then donned his robes. He asked Erin and Chris, a young sister and brother pair from America, to do the readings in English, and then he conducted the Mass for a handful of pilgrims under the azure blue sky. It was one of those truly holy moments. I had been to a few Masses while walking, mostly because I needed a quiet place to gather myself, and was angered many times by the vulgarity of the wealth while I was sitting in these tiny churches in the hinterlands of Spain. I often felt that it would be more 'real' to have church outside without all that gaudiness, and there we were, after an exceptionally emotional experience, having Mass on top of a mountain.

My all-time favourite bible scripture is Luke 12:6–7. Jesus was speaking to his disciples, and he said, 'Are not five sparrows sold for two pennies? Yet not one of them is forgotten by God. Indeed, the very hairs of your head are all numbered. Don't be afraid; you are worth more than many sparrows.' Each day, the Catholic Church has the same scripture readings globally, and Erin has an app whereby she can follow the readings in English. As Pablo conducted the Mass and I read the app with her, I saw that this was the scripture on that day, and I simply wept. I could not doubt that the Universe was clearly speaking to me. This scripture confirmed what I had felt under the cross as I lay down my stones representing fear and uncertainty.

I cannot say that this is why I was called to walk the Camino, but I have no doubt that I needed to be in exactly that place at that moment to receive that message. I am just filled with awe and wonder! The space within me seems to be expanding more than I can hold, and all I can say is, 'Watch out world!' I have also decided to continue walking once I get to Santiago, which will not be on my birthday but the day after. I will continue to Finisterre to experience the end of the world. I figure, what is another 90 kilometres in the scheme of things?

Love and greetings from Barbadelo,

Angie

The Fifth Letter from Negreira, Spain

From: Angela Barnard, making_hay@yahoo.co.uk
To: Dear Friends
Subject: My ode to joy
Date: Thursday, 24 July 2014, 23:24

This past Tuesday saw me awaking one year and one day older and 20.1 kilometres from Santiago de Compostela. The past week has been an incredibly strange one on the Camino. The pilgrims that had walked for long distances suddenly felt chased. In Sarria, hundreds of new pilgrims joined The Way, and the path quite literally felt like a four-lane superhighway. If one walks the last 100 kilometres, one can claim a certificate in Santiago stating that one has 'completed' the Camino. This is the speedy version, and thousands do it each year.

The attitudes of these people are different. They are experiencing a first week when most are experiencing a last week. They generally seem to want to run to Santiago, and it seems quite normal to be inconsiderate, loud and surgically attached to mobile phones. I conditioned myself to be non-judgemental, not to become irritable and simply to allow everyone the freedom to do The Way Their Way. However, I did feel chased and found that my walking speed dramatically increased.

The tradition is to reach Santiago, go directly to the cathedral and attend the twelve o'clock Pilgrims' Mass. I really wanted to do this so I found myself departing at 6 a.m. on Tuesday morning to walk to Santiago. When I left, in the dark, a large pitch-black forest immediately confronted me that I needed to traverse. I had no lamp worth writing about, and, in my near-blindness, was unable to cross this forest alone. So I insinuated myself into a group of flying Spaniards and felt like I was on a broomstick whizzing through the forest in the dark. When that forest ended, another began, and the fun continued. I was walking excessively fast for my chubby legs to carry me and eventually had to drop out of the race, but by then I was almost out of the woods.

When I parted from the noisy, flying Spaniards, left abruptly to my own devices, I realised that the journey I had begun in France five weeks earlier was ending. Many events of the past weeks flashed through my mind. I saw people I had walked with go by. I reheard stories I was told. I remembered pain and limitations I had overcome. I remembered tears cried in empathy, sorrow and joy. I remembered massages given and received, blisters popped for and by others, bellyaching laughs and moments of frivolous hilarity. I remembered labyrinths walked, pictures taken – both those taken with a camera and those imprinted on the mind.

I marvelled at the lessons learnt, the angels who visited me, the guides who accompanied me and the new family of friends I carry with me for eternity. I also felt and relived the love I had received from all my friends and family everywhere, willing me on, pushing me forward. I was literally buzzing with gratitude and marvelling at this wonderful journey that I have had the pleasure and privilege to travel.

Coming to Monte do Gozo, a hill 5 kilometres from Santiago, and seeing the city for the first time, I was overawed with emotion. It was as if I had the ancestors of the Camino standing before me, the millions still to walk The Way standing behind me, and there I was in the middle, a part of a story that spans centuries and will continue for many to come. The dominant emotions I felt were pure unadulterated gratitude, love and joy. Even now as I try to describe the feelings I am speechless once more and know I shall never be able to express them eloquently.

I made my way into the city limits and began the hard slog, on pavement, to the cathedral. Strangely enough, after the forest experience I was mostly alone during this last walk. In a way, I felt cocooned in a bubble of my own. When I saw the towers of the cathedral for the first time, I burst out laughing, but still it remained hidden and secretive to me, so onward I slogged, hoping to reach my goal. The streets were narrow and winding in the old city, filled with shoppers, cars, and delivery trucks offloading goods for the holy day on the 25th. A hectic mishmash, with the constant stream of pilgrims pressing onwards.

Drawing nearer to what I thought might be the cathedral, I heard the most beautiful music playing. It was crystal clear, and as I drew nearer, I realised it was a flute. The musician was playing something similar to the soundtrack from the movie *The Mission*. Suddenly, Beethoven's 'Ode to Joy' filled my ears. In that moment, it was the soundtrack to my life. I had copious tears rolling down my cheeks, and, as I passed the street musician, I paid him a tribute of both my thanks and money. I was completely filled with boundless joy. When I saw the cathedral, I raised my arms in the air. This was it!

I had time before Mass and made my way to the Pilgrim's Reception Office to obtain my Compostela. As I was standing in line, dear Jürg came along. We fell into each other's arms, crying with joy. I gathered myself together, and, when it was my turn to present my passport and credentials in the office, I was once again overcome. The man behind the counter said, 'You have walked a long way,' to which I just dissolved into ugly-cry mode. I could barely get myself together. But for him, it was as if he had seen this a million times before.

I went into the cathedral and found a seat for the Mass. A nun came into the altar area and led the congregation in song. She had a clear soprano voice that rang out across the cathedral. The bellows of the gorgeous organ accompanied her, and I thought if ever the Catholic Church captured a moment of drama perfectly, this was it. It was like sitting at Heaven's gate and just hearing the creation of God unfold. Of course, I could not understand a word of the Mass, like all the others I attended, but I did not care. That moment was all about my just revelling in joy and gratitude for the wonderful life I felt blessed to have. There was a sense of boundless camaraderie amongst all the pilgrims, friends and strangers alike. We all knew this was a life-changing experience that simply needed to be lived.

The *Botafumeiro*, a giant incense burner used to fumigate the pilgrims back in the day, was not swung that day. Even though I missed this experience, I felt satisfied with everything else. On Wednesday morning, I awoke early to meet and greet other friends who were arriving. It was like experiencing a homecoming of joy. By chance, I popped into the cathedral at 12:30 p.m. and had the wonderful pleasure of watching the *Botafumeiro* being swung to the rafters. I loved the awed gasps of the congregation as it swung close to the ceiling. Actually, it seemed to be more a fireball than an incense ball, but still it was a wonderful experience, especially with the organ dramatically bellowing out what seemed like the soundtrack to a horror movie, and the nun melodiously chanting in Latin!

I decided not to hang around in Santiago for the festival, as I felt called to continue walking to the 'end of the earth', Finisterre. I have begun this journey today. I believe the Camino Francés was about leaving things behind and that the Camino Finisterre is about picking things up. Either way, I remain open and will walk with a grateful heart regardless of the outcome.

Love and blessings from Negreira,

Angie

The Sixth Letter from Finisterre, Spain

From: Angela Barnard, making_hay@yahoo.co.uk
To: Dear Friends
Subject: Reaching the 'end of the world' and the fullness of me
Date: Sunday, 27 July 2014, 19:35

Thursday morning, bright and early, I left the city limits of Santiago de Compostela with my fellow pilgrims Donna and Phil. We were heading to Finis Terrae, the end of the world, 90 kilometres away. After the hectic arrival in Santiago, a city in full celebration, it was wonderful to sneak out at dawn the only pilgrims on The Way, to a cacophony of mad dogs announcing our departure.

What was immediately apparent was how different this part of The Way was, compared to The Way to Santiago. The track was deserted – for many kilometres we were the only pilgrims. The climate was subtropical and humid. There were many vicious little hills, and the track was quite treacherous in places. The vegetation was vastly different. We walked through ancient and young pine forests, followed by woods of giant eucalyptus with wild fern underbrush. We passed many dairy farms, and the humidity and low-hanging mist were constant companions.

I decided to break this journey into four days instead of the recommended three, and, for me, this was the right decision. Over these four days, I found myself walking with a gigantic smile on my face most of time. I carried 'Ode to Joy' in my heart and found that I had to whistle at a high volume quite often. Yesterday I had the privilege of walking 30 kilometres in absolute silence as I was the only pilgrim along The Way. Until that point, I had not experienced such utter aloneness, but I loved every minute of it. I was having an absolute blast; the pine trees were applauding my progress, and the wind carried my laughter up into their boughs.

It is only now that I can say with certainty that I was called to walk the Camino. For all you who know me, you know that I would never willingly submit to such madness and physical torment. I do not sit around dreaming up walking, cycling or running anywhere for anything! I never dreamt of doing the Camino, I never secretly desired to put it on my bucket list. In fact, I think two dear friends who really do want to do this are out of their friggin' trees! When, on 20 May 2014, I first uttered the words to my niece, 'Bee, I think I am going to walk the Camino,' I was shocked and horrified by what came out of my mouth. I am even more astounded but totally blessed that I immediately answered my soul's desire and submitted myself to the madness, beginning an incredible odyssey on 18 June.

A few days before I left home, I had a coaching session with my dear friend and coach Barbara Anderson. In that session, we set a powerful and possibly terrifying goal for my Camino. As I uttered the words of the goal, my head was screaming, *What the fuck! What if you do not achieve this goal?!*, but every ounce of my being knew that it was right for me. Immediately afterwards, I phoned my aunt in Cape Town. I told her of the journey I was about to embark on, and she said, 'Well, my girl, I hope you find what you're looking for.' I mean ... really! The only thing I was looking for was the closing episode of that season's *Game of Thrones*! But as she said it, I immediately said, 'No, Aunty, I hope that whatever's looking for me finds me!' In a way, it was a challenge to the Universe and a true desire. I mean, how the friggin' hell was I going to achieve my goal without a little help?

I am reminded of a conversation I had with dear Juan, weeks ago, about why we were walking the Camino. There we were, plodding along, and I told him all this, and he said, with absolute certainty, 'What belongs to us is ours.' I stopped dead in my tracks, stood gaping at him, and said, 'Where did that come from?' He said, 'I don't know,' and we were both struck by the absolute clarity, certainty and truth of that statement. Backpacks and all, we embraced and cried together, and then we continued along. We have both quoted this truth to one another. Juan, I want you to know that I have what is mine.

Walking to Santiago was about letting go of things – exactly what, I am not 100 per cent sure, because most of the time I walked in the now. I know that it is not my problem to worry about it. Walking to Finisterre was about picking things up. On Friday morning, I was alone, and I asked, 'What is mine, and how do I get it?' And the answer came, 'You simply take what is yours.' So what is mine, and what was I looking for? What is mine is who I really am and accepting that. I know that sounds ludicrous, but the truth is that I have had an amazing life and am an amazing person with some exceptional gifts, but I have never really accepted them. I have doubted the gifts I have been given, and this has prevented me from taking the steps I need to live my dreams. I have created lies or listened to them, hidden behind barriers and fears, doubted myself. I have been in a holding pattern.

I know that the shit storm I lived through earlier this year is the Universe's way of setting me free from the drudgery of a life lived unfulfilled. Since I can remember, it has been my heart's desire to live my best life, to let my symphony ring out loud and clear, and to help others achieve this as well. I have always known this is what I must do, but I have stood in my own way. Therefore, by coming to accept who I am and stepping into the fullness of this, I hope I can move forward. As I was walking along and seeing myself for who I really was, I experienced a sense of fullness and wholeness unknown to me before.

So what does this actually mean for me practically? I am going to follow my calling and work as a coach – for which I have already studied. I want to set up my own business and see where it leads me. I also feel that somewhere within me there is a story that needs telling, and I want to write it. I am content in the knowledge that if I could walk 900 kilometres without the slightest natural inclination, my God what else I can do?!

I want to thank my Camino family for being a part of my journey and process. Many times you shared your feedback with me and told me how you saw me. You saw me as kind and gentle and a connector of people. My humour made some days more bearable and my wisdom often brought clarity and insight to many I walked with. It was so hard to hear and accept, but I thank you. I am truly humbled by the love and care that I have received from you guys.

Earlier on the Camino I was often awestruck by my shadow that would go before me as the sun rose. For me, my shadow came to symbolise not that which is without but rather that which is within. I have a giant within. We all do! Just waiting to burst forth. This is not something outside of ourselves but is within and intrinsically ours. It cannot be diminished and is ever present. Without me, there is no shadow and without it there is no me … Almost six weeks ago, I began this journey. I have left my sweat, tears and, today, my blood as I fell along The Way. I have felt the pull of the Camino ancestors; I have seen the hopes and fears of those who are still to come. I am now part of the Camino history and spirit – I too have become an ancestor. Today I met the place where in ancient times they believed the world ended. Where the earth ended, the sky and sea began, the unknown awaited. There I stood myself, knowing and accepting who I really am.

Love and blessings from Finis Terrae,

Angie

The Seventh Letter from Angers, France

From: Angela Barnard, making_hay@yahoo.co.uk
To: Dear Friends
Subject: Last thoughts from a homeward-bound pilgrim
Date: Wednesday, 30 July 2014, 19:21

Yesterday afternoon, I arrived back in Saint-Jean-Pied-de-Port at the same time of the day as when I arrived there six weeks before. I fetched my car keys, checked on my car, and discovered that there was not a scratch, not a bump, not a drop of bird crap on it. In fact, she looked cleaner than when I parked her. She must have been extremely happy to see me because she started first time after standing untouched for six weeks. I just laughed, because I knew that was how things were going to be. I checked into the same *albergue* I had stayed in when this journey began and received exactly the same bed, coming full circle.

As I was returning by bus to Saint-Jean-Pied-de-Port, I was thinking of all the many steps I had taken in the opposite direction. I saw many of the places I had walked, and new pilgrims on The Way. Seeing the Pyrenees again filled me with dread, but I remembered that I had conquered that molehill six weeks prior with Brendan's help. Of course I thoroughly enjoyed regaling the new pilgrims on the bus with stories of the hell and torment they were about to face.

With all of the thoughts, analyses, remembrances, smiles, laughs and tears, I was wondering what was the one thing, if choosing just one thing was possible, that touched or affected me the most on The Way. If you would indulge me one more time, I would like to tell you another story as I conclude these pilgrim missives. This is undoubtedly the story/challenge/message that moves me to tears each time I think of it (of him), and, even as I write, I am once again filled with emotion as I know what this means for my life.

In León, I met two real 'tarts'. These two women openly advertised their tartiness by wearing matching bright-pink Lycra sleeveless shirts that said, 'I'm walking with that tart →' and '← I'm walking with that tart.' When I saw them from a distance, I just smiled and thought, 'Mmm, South African tarts!' as this is a lovingly insulting term South Africans use. When one of them sat down on the bed next to mine and started spouting forth in a beautiful Durban accent like mine, I was delighted! Val, the Durbanite, lives in Cape Town, and she was walking with Jean, the other tart, who's also from Cape Town. In the second it took me to open my heart to them I knew these two were gems. As is the spirit and tradition of the Camino, we bonded very quickly, and within moments we were Camino family.

Val and I sat hunched on our beds. Few bottom bunks are high enough to sit on properly. This, for those of you doing the Camino one day, is important to know: the bunk beds are more suitable for the size-impaired people of the world, and the global healthcare industry benefits greatly from retuning pilgrims with neck and back problems! However, let me not digress … Val said to me, 'You know, Angie, I have come to realise that so many parents waste their time repeating the mistakes of their parents, cramming and forcing rubbish on their children. The one thing I truly did right in my life was teaching my son from a small boy to live his own truth.'

Her son, Wade, grasped this early on in life, and, when she would start nagging about inconsequential, nonsensical stuff, he would always say, 'Mom, none of that is important.' Wade was always busy and seldom had time for her, and she always asked him what he was up to, what was so important, and why must he be running around. He would answer, 'Mom, one day you will understand.' He finally gave her a day all to herself, just the two of them – the day before he died in a car accident at eighteen years of age.

Val finally understood the morning 600 people arrived at the beach to surf his funeral reef out to sea. Later that afternoon, over 1,000 people gathered on the beach to celebrate his life in memorial, and countless numbers of them told Val how Wade had affected their lives. She knew then that in his briefest time on earth he had truly lived a full life and had lived his own truth.

Does the story affect me because it is tragic that Wade died so young or because Val lost a beloved son or because I am turning into an emotional lump? No, I do not think so. I am moved because I know without a doubt that we all are required to seek joy and live joyous lives. I've seen how I've wasted time on stupid inconsequential things that didn't bring me joy and how I haven't always lived my truth. I know that it is not easy to do.

Sometimes our own personal truth is judged and condemned by others. It is in conflict with what others, or even what we ourselves, might think to be true. Surely when we live our truth then we are truly free? I believe that a government, a parent, a partner, a society, a job, a church, does not give freedom to us. It comes from being true to our calling and ourselves and living our lives joyfully in the pursuit of that truth. For those of us who are older, it means dropping the baggage. For those of us who are younger, it means not picking the baggage up. It also requires living consciously and not falling into a holding pattern of unawareness. So, along with all the hundreds of other lessons I have learnt, this is the one that I will carry with me: Angela, live your own truth.

Of course I knew this before I walked the Camino, but it was not alive to me, not on a cellular level. Thank you Val for allowing Wade to remind me of this truth. I hope everyone reading this will also be able to live their own truths, whatever they may be.

Love and blessings from Angers, France,

Angie

A BRIEF INTERLUDE

'Tell me a story.' – Valentina Earp-Jones

A Journal Entry Four Days after Returning

Tuesday, 5 August 2014, 7:15 a.m.

It's a week today since I started travelling home, and it feels rather sad. This is the first time in the longest, longest while that I remember feeling discombobulated after travelling. I feel a sense of emptiness. It's not so much a comedown as a void which I seem to have – and a longing for The Way. It feels like I've left a very dear and old friend behind, and I want to go back and say, 'Hey, I haven't deserted you, I'm just somewhere else.' I know it sounds crazy, but I feel a kind of jealousy for the new pilgrims that are walking. I know I had my own adventures, my own breakthroughs, insights, breakdowns, homesickness, physical illness, challenges, and euphoria, but some part of me wants more.

When I stood in Finisterre, I knew the journey had ended. It felt completed. I remember looking into the endlessness of the horizon, and I knew that all that lay before me was mine and I could inhabit it in freedom and with joy. However, at the back of my mind, I don't feel like The Way is finished with me.

Of course I know that it's after such an adventure that the processing kicks in, the remembrances, lessons, regrets, aches, joys, etc., but what I didn't expect was this sense of deep longing. Longing for what? Walking? Not really. I don't feel a great urge to put on my shoes and go walking here. Is it the freedom and the lack of responsibility, the stimulation, the group therapy, the camaraderie, the routine that I miss? Do I miss the pilgrims' meals, the uncomfortable beds? The public showers? (*HELL, NO!*) The mass of human bodies all scrambling to get ready in the dark each morning?

I don't think I miss any of these things. What I think I'm missing is setting off every morning to accompany The Way. I miss the cacophony of birdsong, the morning breeze, the stillness of dawn and the evil wicked flies that disturb one's peace. I miss hearing 'Buen Camino!' While I was not always fully aware of it, I think I miss the energy of The Way. There is an energy there, which opens your mind, soul, heart, and spirit. It allows you to be one with all. For me, it brought a sense of harmony and balance.

I also experienced a great sense of resolution on The Way. There was a drive – an incessant drive – not to give up! When the pain was overwhelming or The Way too long or the sun too hot or the rain too driving or the wind too gusty, there was always this push and pull: Don't give up! Continue! Yes, you can!

I wonder if The Way gives each person that which they are looking for or that which they need? Is it possible that there is such power there, such energy, that the Universe knows exactly how to deal with each person individually? For me, it was less about St James and God and more about The Way. This was simply how it felt to me. An energy vein coursing through northern Spain that attracts unwitting travellers and spits them out at the other end ... different.

On the forums, I have been seeing pictures of pilgrims I met. They all look totally different at the end to how they looked when I met them. Many seem to possess a new-found lightness, a glow, an inner depth. I know from my pictures that I too look different. I also seem to glow and have depth – whatever that might mean! LOL.

Who would have thought? I really do not understand the pull I am feeling to go back. In fact, I don't even feel any of my natural resistance. It's a feeling of an old friend waiting to welcome me back to their home. Will I heed the call? The German has changed her mind about cycling the Camino and has said that she would like to walk it. I have told her that if she does I would go with her if she wants me to. Am I out of my tree? I don't think so! LOL.

Perhaps this is just the jitters one feels after being away from home a long time. I know I need to reflect each day on The Way and on my experience of it. I know I must not panic but just allow myself to feel and to go with the flow. All is well and will continue to be well. I want to volunteer my time to work in some capacity along The Way, and I will action this soon.

A Few Thoughts

Subject: The Endless Way …
Date: Wednesday, 22 April 2015, 17:32

Months have passed since I returned home and wrote that journal entry. Did my longing subside? Did things return to 'normal'? Hell no! When the vivid, technicolour dreams started in which I would quite literally hear the Camino calling my name, I, at first, thought I was going mad. I would wake out of a dream and feel the urge to put on my hiking clothes and start walking in the direction of Spain.

I researched the phenomenon of the deep longing to return, and it seems that the majority of returning pilgrims have this experience. I concluded that it was my soul's longing for my best self. This is who I experienced along The Way, my best me. I was one with everything; I had limitless compassion and love for everything; patience was my first, middle and last name. I was totally in flow and expanding to the limitless potential of all that is and can be. These are lessons I take with me each day, and I try to remain present in the moment and allow the full potential of life to be mine.

Returning home, I felt like a fish out of water. How does one explain to others who have no similar frame of reference what walking 900 kilometres does to a person? I felt the limitless potential of everything on a microscopic level, and I was highly attuned to the wastage of this potential, which seemed so prevalent. I was acutely aware of everything around me: nature, people, machinery, the hustle and bustle of life, and I tried not to become consumed by it all. I was aware that my environment had not yet expanded to accept the evolving me, and I did not want to return to my old ways.

We have a stone Zen-style garden with small shrubs and a fish pond. I often missed the absence of bird life in our garden. When I returned home, I was delighted to see that a gang of sparrows had taken up residence in my neighbour's shrubs. I asked if I had been so clueless previously as not to notice them, but I was reassured that this gang had taken up residence while I was walking. I wrote earlier about the message of the sparrow and returned home to find a small miracle had occurred reminding me of my encounters with sparrows along The Way. As the biggest challenge I had to overcome was not believing in and accepting myself, I had to laugh when I saw them. I knew they had been sent to me as ever-present reminders. And my God did they rise to the challenge!

Before I embarked upon The Way, I had a specialised career as a flavourist with one of the largest global flavour houses, which creates flavours and fragrances for some of the world's leading food and cosmetic brands. This career afforded me many wonderful opportunities, but I was not happy for the longest time. The problem with being highly specialised is that one becomes accustomed to a certain lifestyle, and this was true for me, so I continued in my unhappiness 'making a living' but not really living in joy. I wanted to be working with people, reaching my full potential and helping others do the same. In 2006, I made this random, grand statement to the universe and all around me: 'I am going to become a life coach.' This took me by surprise as I had never been coached, neither did I know any coaches, and yet here I was making this proclamation. Shortly thereafter, I transferred to Germany with the company I was working for and a few months later to Singapore, and it was there that I seized the opportunity to study as a life coach.

I worked for this flavour house for fifteen years and in 2012 decided to change companies and work for the competition. It was at that company that I experienced workplace bullying and became ill from the trauma of that experience. I simply could not continue to work in a sick environment and accepted a settlement package from them that afforded me the space and time to heal myself and consider my next move. Healing was my top priority, and as part of that process I visited my niece in Canada where I once again made a crazy proclamation, with no forethought: 'I am going to walk the Camino.'

As I walked the Camino, these thoughts were present with me. What do I want to do with my life? Can I take this risk? Would I believe in myself and my many talents? Do I want to start living instead of earning a living? It was in O Cebreiro on Day 27 of my walk that I first uttered the words, 'I am going to start my own business and work as a coach.' I said this to two strangers from Boston over dinner. The woman thought I was starting a cult and began telling me of her brother's experiences with cults in California. I mean … really! Coaching and culting are in no way similar or related … although some days I do wonder!

It didn't matter. What was important was that I had set the intention; those words I had uttered in 2006 were now becoming reality. Talk about overcoming fear and stepping out of a comfort zone! Nevertheless, this is what I had been doing since I returned home. I founded my company, Inspire for Life Coaching, and, Ye Gods, what a ride.

I had never been self-employed, and it was a gigantic learning curve for me. I had studied business management, but it does not give you the real-life tools of being able to find your voice and niche as a business owner. So there were moments of insecurity, doubt and fear. Unbelievably it was in those moments that gang of sparrows popped up screeching their heads off, reminding me of what I knew for sure.

On 21 August 2014, a few weeks after returning home, I went walking in the forest near my home. I needed to make decisions and was digging myself into a hole of uncertainty and doubt. Shortly after entering the forest, I felt that I should sit on a bench instead of walking as I intended. I was doing that nonsense of spinning around in circles in my head, and I took a brief moment to become still and ask for clarity. From the undergrowth opposite the bench came such a cacophony of bird noise one could have imagined that a dangerous enemy was passing nearby. I peered into the bushes, trying to make out what the fuss was about, when I noticed a little sparrow screeching and hopping around from branch to branch. If there are drama queens in the sparrow kingdom, I can guarantee that this was one of them. I got the distinct impression that this little guy was yelling at me, and I just smiled, remembering the lessons I had learnt. *Don't be afraid, Angie, you are worth more than many sparrows. Remember: the very hairs of your head are all numbered.* Not good enough for the little sparrow, oh no! He hopped out of the bush onto the pathway, faced me directly and really turned up the volume. This little guy had a message for me: How dare I not pay attention! How dare I forget! I sat on that bench and cackled like a madwoman.

After I remembered not to forget and reconnected to my centre, I left the forest and returned home.

When I arrived home, I checked my phone, and there was a message from Donna in Portland, Oregon: 'Sending good thoughts your way. Hope you are having a good day.'

'Received. Just what I needed. Am having another floppy with myself.'

'You are not going to believe this. There was a sparrow trapped in our library. Lisa and I caught it, took it outside, and set it free.'

'How awesome!'

'We were thinking of you. Obviously, you were thinking of us and sent the sparrow to start a crazy registration day!'

While I was not thinking of my pilgrim sisters, Donna and Lisa, as I was in the forest, somehow they received a message to think of me and send me love.

If the message wasn't already firmly embedded, I was sent another powerful message on Sunday, 14 September 2014. It was a glorious evening, and I was Skyping with Roy and Sylvia in Los Angeles. I was going out to dinner with my friend Marion that night, and she came over and joined me on the sofa as we wrapped up our conversation online. Sylvia said she wanted to give me some feedback on our chat, and this is what she then said: 'It sounds to me that living your own truth has become your biggest thing. All of us are trying to find our truth, and what the Camino gave you is that sense of what your role is in this world, and you're now defining what that means to you. You are transitioning, going deeper into self-belief, and you are allowing yourself to trust your instinct. Get away from your fear of not facing your truth. This means getting rid of things that stop you. You do have that gift of being able to write, so you need to start writing little snippets and start sending them out to the world. People from anywhere in the world are going to come to you, and you need to allow them to take the lessons that only you can teach and share. It's a master class of self-discovery, and you are going to be a master teacher, you understand. And your sparrow is going to be your picture and your guide, your image of you. Therefore, you need to get someone to draw it or paint it for you. OK?'

Our living room where we were sitting directly overlooks the garden and patio. The door was open to allow the beautiful evening in, and at the exact moment that Sylvia mentioned the sparrow, a little bird alighted on the handrail next to the door. She was facing into the house, and she proceeded to literally screech at us. Marion began beating my leg in excitement pointing exuberantly at the little gal. I sat there like a gaping fish wondering if I was experiencing a parallel universe. What I actually 'heard' in my head from that little bird was, 'Angela! You walked that shit out of you!'

Messages don't come clearer than that. Oh, I've had my moments of doubt and fear and worry, but I haven't allowed myself to get stuck there. I've continued moving forward, letting go of stuff, allowing myself to *be* who I am, allowing my truth to prevail. The Way is never completed. It's not an experience that I lived for thirty-four days somewhere in Spain in my forty-seventh year on Earth. The lessons remain engrained within, profoundly changing my attitude towards life. Many things I 'knew' before I now KNOW for sure.

I know that I don't need possessions to make me happy.

I know that simplicity is what suits me best.

I know that self-expression, love, compassion and gratitude are my compass.

I know that the dimensions of my potential are boundless.

I know that I can accomplish anything I set my mind to.

I know that what I found is not what I was looking for; it is far greater than my limited imagination could conceive.

I know that I will walk again.

Love and blessings from Holzminden,

Angie

A Letter from My Camino First Love

From: Brendan Kelly, brendantkelly1@gmail.com
To: Dear Camino Family
Subject: My first Camino
Date: Friday, 22 May 2015, 19:08

Dear Camino Family,

I am not a writer. In fact, in all my years I wouldn't need both hands to count the number of letters I have written. It is only in the past few years that I have started to use email. At the end of March when I had finished the Camino Primitivo, the lovely Angela Barnard asked me a few questions about the Primitivo, and I told her I would give her an update. I then saw Angela's post on Facebook yesterday, and I thought I'd better respond before I incur her wrath. Trying to write about the walk, however, I feel I have to explain what drew me to my second Camino, and, of course, the experience of my first Camino and its effect on me. So, here goes, for those that may be interested.

In 2011, my life was good. I was living on the outskirts of beautiful Sydney, Australia, with Nancy, my wife. I emigrated from Scotland to Australia in 1972, and, after thirty-nine years, we were in a comfortable position with no mortgage and both earning a good living. We had the big European adventure planned for June 2011 when, at the end of May, Nancy fell ill. I won't go into detail about her heroics, courage and suffering, except to say that she died on 30 January 2012, just after her sixty-third birthday. I was devastated. How could this be? I am the one who smokes, drinks and doesn't exercise. It should have been me.

My life changed. My wife, my lover, my best friend, had gone, and she wasn't coming back. I would go to work and not want to go home. When I eventually did go home, I would make a meal, put it on the table, sit down and look at Nancy's empty chair. I would then shove the food aside, open another bottle of wine, and go and sit in the garden, drinking wine, smoking cigarettes, looking at the night sky and talking to myself.

'How did this happen?'

'Why did it happen?'

'Did I do everything I could to prevent this?'

'Can you hear me Nancy?'

'Do you have a soul?'

'Is there a God?'

'Fuck you, God!'

'I am sorry, God, forgive me.'

I would be sobbing; I didn't know that you could miss someone so much. Always feeling sorry – not for me, but for Nancy: she had so much to live for. I was confused. This must happen to half the population at some time in their life. I am weak; I have to be strong for my grief-stricken son and daughter.

'Have another drink, Brendan, maybe sleep will come tonight.'

Eight months after Nancy, my youngest brother died – another victim of cancer. I felt drained and empty. My son and daughter suggested that I needed a change. My son said, 'Dad, you have always wanted to spend some time in Europe. Travel, Dad, just do it.' I quit my job, left my house in the hands of a real-estate agent to rent and arrived in Scotland in March 2014, where I bought a motorhome/RV.

Why did I walk the Camino Francés? It all started by chance. Although I have always enjoyed the outdoors, I was never a hiker. The last time I was in Scotland with Nancy, we were driving down through the Scottish Highlands from the Isle of Skye to Glen Coe, and I could see people walking through the mist and wet heather. I commented to her, 'Look at those crazy people, do you think they are enjoying themselves?' Nancy replied, 'I am sure they are. They are walking on the West Highland Way.' She then said that it was something she would like to do the next time she visited Scotland. That was OK with me, and I told her I would meet her at the end of every stage.

Just before I left Australia, my daughter and I were taking Nancy's clothes to the charity shop. Nancy had a The North Face Gore-Tex jacket, and my daughter said, 'This will fit you, Dad.'

I replied, 'It's a ladies jacket.'

'It's a unisex jacket, Dad, put it on,' she said. I did, and at that moment I knew I had to walk the West Highland Way for Nancy.

When I was researching the West Highland Way on the Internet, Google would regularly bring up the Camino, one of the world's great walks. I was thinking, *An 800-kilometre pilgrimage? I don't think so. If I walked the Camino, it would be an adventure and not a pilgrimage. Let's see how I go on the West Highland Way first.*

Wearing Nancy's jacket to keep Scotland's miserable weather at bay, I walked the 160-kilometre West Highland Way. For me, it was a physically tough, exhilarating, historic walk through some of Scotland's best scenery, and I am sure I could hear Nancy's commentary all the way. However, the fact that she wasn't with me just made me feel melancholy and sad.

I felt physically better after walking the West Highland Way and decided to try to walk the Camino. I thought it would be an adventure and that I could do with losing a few more pounds. From day one I met wonderful, unforgettable people. Chris, sensible hat and sandals. Erin with flowers in her hair. Super-fit Nina who stopped walking to see if I was OK when I was seriously out of breath. The effervescent Angela when we were both struggling on that first day. We shared lunch and thoughts and then walked down the mountain feeling much better together. This meeting of caring, sharing people continued for the duration of the Camino, and they are all etched in my memory.

I met many people on the walk, and I never met anyone I did not like – except one guy. I met him in a café bar, while I was replacing a Compeed on my heel. He told me that he had been on the Camino many times and that the way I was doing it was all wrong. I didn't say anything, which is unusual for me, and I just listened. 'Your backpack is too big, your boots are too heavy, and you are wearing the wrong type of clothes.' His companion interrupted him, saying that they had to leave or they would miss their bus.

'You're catching a bus?' I asked.

His companion replied, 'Yes, it's too hot to walk.'

I laughed aloud, and the companion wished me 'Buen Camino'. I just nodded and didn't reply.

For me, there was something magical happening every other day, which I should record before dementia gets the better of me. I was, however, still in a self-destruct mode, not caring about myself. Outwardly, I would laugh and joke with people; inwardly, I was scared of being alone in the evening with my depressive thoughts and would usually be the last person to go to bed, trying to avoid the black cloud of depression.

I had carried a small flat stone, which I could write on, from Nancy's favourite beach in Scotland. I had thought, *This is all voodoo*, but it is Camino tradition, and I get the symbolism of losing weight, so why not? When I reached Cruz de Ferro, I left the inscribed stone and was immediately overcome with emotion. I wept uncontrollably for God knows how long. When I left Cruz de Ferro, my overweight backpack felt like a bubble on my back, and I floated down the hill.

I was feeling good walking towards Monte do Gozo when I saw a familiar face. It was my friend, Eddie, from Scotland, who had flown in to walk the last few miles with me. Eddie is a serious hiker and has walked all over the UK but had never had the time to walk the Camino. We talked for a while and then started walking into Santiago. Suddenly, I stopped walking. I felt as if I had an epiphany. I am sure I could hear Nancy saying to me, 'Wake up to yourself, you have a lot to live for,' and I could hear myself saying aloud, 'Yeah, yes, you're right, I do!'

Eddie asked if I was OK. I told him everything was fine. I went to Santiago, partied for a few days with Marina and Cyril and then on to Finisterre to burn some socks and my stupid hat. In Finisterre, I met Donna DeLuca, who I had first met on a bench in front of the León Cathedral (I think I was feeling sorry for myself) and who was very comforting. When I saw her face in Finisterre, it just made me smile. Life was good.

I had intended to go to Muxia, but the partying in Santiago and Finisterre had taken its toll, and my old hips said, 'Enough.' My Camino was finished. I caught buses back to Saint-Jean-Pied-de-Port to my motorhome and enjoyed meandering up the coast of France and eventually back to Scotland for Christmas.

It was a new year, and something was bugging me. I was missing the Camino. Why didn't I go to Muxia? Was it something in that movie, *The Way*, about the father reconnecting with his dead son, who had to go on to Muxia, without a blister in sight? I had to go back. I decided I wanted to do a shorter, tough, winter walk. The Camino Primitivo, at 320 kilometres, seemed perfect.

The solitude, scenery and silence of Asturias are beautiful. Being at the end of winter, I only met three people on the walk: one young man, who was recovering from a relationship break-up, and a married couple who walk every couple of years, just to clear their minds. They asked me why I was walking. I told them I had walked the Camino Francés last year and that it had saved me from myself but that I regretted not going on to Muxia. The Primitivo was a great hike. I got to Santiago feeling great, but the urge to walk to Muxia had gone. I fetched my motorhome and drove to Muxia.

At the end of the Camino Francés, I had posted a thank-you to my Camino friends on Facebook and said that my Camino was over. The wise Juan Alberto

Lopez Uribe correctly replied in a comment, 'The Camino is not over, Brendan. This is just the beginning ... ' I assume we all had different reasons for doing the Camino and therefore expected different outcomes. I had no expectations.

My friends, many of you have said that you miss the Camino and that you may walk another one. If you do, I am sure you will enjoy it, but, as Sylvia Nilsen said in Angela's Facebook post, 'There is nothing quite like the first.' For me, it was the first Camino that will have the lasting memory. Maybe if the Primitivo was my first Camino I might have a different opinion; however, I doubt it. It was more than thirty days, almost four weeks, before I had my so-called epiphany, and I would have finished the Primitivo by then. But who knows?

The Primitivo was a great, exhilarating hike, and I often felt as one with nature and made some great, lifelong friends. But it is the Camino Francés and the unforgettable people I met on The Way that saved me from myself and gave me the will to live and enjoy life to the full. I am enjoying life now, and when I am somewhere I know Nancy would love, it makes me smile.

Love to all,

Brendan

A Journal Entry on the Day of Departure

Monday, 16 June 2014, 06:25

I will sing, sing a new song. I will sing, sing a new song.

The song I have been singing has been melancholic, depressed and suppressed.

A new song is coming through – one which is pregnant with the expectancy of life, one which is vibrant and full of zest.

A song of refreshment, a song of healing.

A song that will bring joy to my heart and the hearts of those who hear it.

It's a song of clarity and purity, love and joy.

This song is infectious and humorous, boundless in its interpretation. The melody flows, the harmony synchronises.

It's a song of healing and power. As I hear it and sing it, I am empowered, and those who hear me sing it are empowered.

Thank you, Spirit, for this new song.

I will sing, sing a new song!

This Was 'The End'

Isn't it funny how we think something is finished only to discover that it is not? I honestly believed I had finished my little tale about walking the Camino, and I was about to publish it. Something within and distractions without kept causing delays, and I never went to press. As the first anniversary of my walk drew near, I had the idea to write a weekly blog post about the lessons I had learnt from the Camino. I was feeling a very strong affinity and connection to the Camino, more so than usual, so I followed through on this impulse, and this is how the story unfolded. You may be thinking, *Oh God, when is this woman going to bring this tale to an end?*, but, as we all know, good stories never end, they just keep on unfolding.

PART II

LESSONS FROM THE WAY

'Life can only be understood backwards; but it must be lived forwards.' — Søren Kierkegaard

Blog Post 1: The Only Way Out Is In

Date: Tuesday, 16 June 2015, 10:15

Today I am celebrating the first anniversary of an epic adventure and journey in my life. I was slowly emerging from a very painful and soul-destroying experience that left me feeling battered and beaten. I did not know my up from my down, felt unrecognisable to myself and, at times, felt like I had reached the end of the line. There was a fantastic support network around me, but my inner numbness and broken spirit did not always allow me to see the extended hands of love reaching in my direction. I experienced extreme restlessness and felt the propensity to leave, that desire to walk out the door and never return. I had one major limitation to following through on that thought: as a well-established, overweight, unfit, couch potato, I was not about to exert so much effort escaping from myself.

In mid-May, I declared, 'I think I'm going to walk the Camino' and felt horrified by the nonsense spewing forth from my mouth. However, twenty-seven days later, at 10 a.m., I left Germany, heading south-west towards the French–Spanish border and arriving at the foot of the Pyrenees the following evening. I had driven 1,829 kilometres and started walking 789 kilometres across Spain the next day.

I was on pilgrimage.

In the short build-up to this unplanned, undesired adventure, I often wondered what the hell was I thinking. Me! Couch Potato Queen of the Universe! Setting off to walk across a foreign country, in the middle of summer, with barely a plan in my head and few muscles in my legs.

The Way of St James, aka the Camino de Santiago, was not something with which I was familiar. I have no religious connections, no close friends who were pilgrims, and I am not prone to extreme vacations. All I had was the compulsion, the drive, the call: 'I've gotta walk. I've gotta go!' Those who were familiar with my circumstances thought I was running away from myself. However, if this were the case, would I not have driven or flown to an exotic location that did not require pain, suffering and excessive exertion on my part? Others thought I was looking for something, and, to some extent, I was, but I also felt that something was looking for me.

In the days prior to my departure, I had strong, mixed emotions. I experienced huge amounts of fear. I did not know what was waiting for me. Would I find shelter? Would I be safe? Would I manage to walk across Spain? What type of people would be along The

Way? Was it unwise to leave behind all electronic gadgets? What if something happened to my health? Would I cope with the exertion? What did the future hold? Would I be disappointed and more broken when I reached Santiago de Compostela? Was the whole venture in vain? What if I found no answers, or my slothful body rebelled and I returned home a failure? While my fears were numerous and varied, I concurrently felt euphoric expectation. I was brimming with it, and, as a somewhat cynical traveller, this buzzing excitement surprised me.

I experienced the first crisis of the soul within 10 kilometres of departure. I literally felt slapped over the head by those majestic Pyrenees mountains and stood breathless, feeling unable to continue. I remember thinking to myself that it was too much to handle. I could not do it alone, and I should hitch a ride or catch a bus or perhaps sit down and weep. Standing there, I asked for help. I said, 'I cannot do this alone. I seriously need help. I need angels, guides, divine intervention, my body, my higher self. I need you all to assist me.' My help was literally around the next bend, showing me clearly that if I ask, I shall receive.

A year ago, I could not fully comprehend what a pilgrimage would entail or even what it meant. I could not grasp the full depth of the journey my body, soul, mind and spirit would undertake. I had no idea of the immense joy I could find, while in pain and suffering, walking 789 kilometres across Spain. Based on my own experience, I do not believe that anyone can undertake a pilgrimage without undergoing major life and attitude changes.

In retrospect, I can say that I was looking for something. I was seeking direction for my life, seeking healing, but, most importantly, I was seeking myself. What I now know for sure is that the only way out is in. So often we want to escape from dreadful situations or look for solutions in trivial distractions. We numb or deflect our pain with substances or modern entertainments. We look to gurus, religion and seek outside advice. We look for the easy way out, but there is none. The way out of anything that causes us pain is to go within ourselves. Not to become a hermit, secluded from the world, but to find our true selves – the essence of who we are.

When we go within, we discover who we are and what we stand for. We begin to know our inner strength and learn from our inner wisdom. By going within, we experience the stillness of our soul, that place where we find full acceptance for who we are. The way out of an unfulfilled life is to go within. It is deep within that we can find our own joy, tap into our innate inspiration and grasp the wonder of our own potential and magnificence.

Today, I look back at the events leading up to my pilgrimage with great joy and gratitude. I marvel that so many wonderful blessings, adventures, lessons and wisdom came from a place of such deep pain and suffering. I look at myself today and simply feel love and self-acceptance. That is what I was seeking. That is what I found. And I know that if I never went within I would never have given myself the gift of me.

I realise that not everyone feels called to walk a pilgrimage or has the resources to do so; however, we do all have the ability to go within, to know ourselves, to love and practise self-acceptance. Whatever your life circumstances, be encouraged to explore your inner treasures. You really are worth it.

Buen Camino!

Blog Post 2: Six Resilience Tips I Learnt Climbing the Pyrenees

Date: Tuesday, 23 June 2015, 10:35

In life, we all have mountains to climb. Some are literal, others figurative. Today I would like to share with you six lessons I learnt climbing the Pyrenees. As you know, the official route of the Camino Francés begins in the little town of Saint-Jean-Pied-de-Port nestled in the foothills of the majestic Pyrenees in France. Driving along the E5 motorway towards Spain, I fell into a fool's dream. The journey seemed so easy, and I wondered what all the fuss was about. Where were the treacherous Pyrenees that pilgrims seemed to fear?

At Bayonne, my navigation informed me that I was 48 kilometres from my destination. There were no mountains in sight. All seemed well. Leaving the motorway, the journey suddenly changed. Driving the narrow winding road, the local drivers seemed impatient, reckless and too fast for my liking. I needed much more alertness and concentration than before and felt stressed for the first time on the journey. The vegetation in that area was very dense, and, for much of the time, it was like driving downward through a thick, green, twisting tunnel. Yet still I wondered, where are the mountains that people seem to fear?

The moment I first saw the Pyrenees I was filled with fear. I felt breathless and nearly crashed my car. I desperately looked for a place to pull over and sat there, staring at my nemesis thinking, 'OH MY GOD! WHAT HAVE I DONE?!' This is where my first lesson began.

1. Choose your response to fear.

My perspective from a distance was very different to my perspective as I reached Saint-Jean-Pied-de-Port. From a distance, the Pyrenees seemed high and frightening. Driving closer, they seemed insurmountable and petrifying. I had to choose my response to fear. I had options: Return home. Catch a bus around the mountain. Break the journey into two days. Or, follow through on my plan and walk over.

A year ago, I was unfit, unhealthy and heavier than I am now. Nobody would have blamed me if I had decided not to try. Actually, the odds were stacked against my succeeding, but I decided to acknowledge my fear and walk with it anyway. I chose not to remain rooted in fear and overwhelmed by the unknown but to walk and with each step to see what could unfold for me. My response was not to allow my fears to immobilise me.

2. Do not compare yourself to others.

Each day, hundreds of pilgrims stream out of Saint-Jean-Pied-de-Port heading towards Spain. There are those that walk at a brisk pace, those that wend and wind their way up, those that jog, those that slog, those that cycle, those riding on horseback, those in wheelchairs – the list is endless. The first 8 kilometres, mildly put, are hell. I watched the other pilgrims finding their stride and began comparing myself to them. Doubts set in; I became worried, fearful and angry. I had a running dialogue in my head that was not supporting my physical efforts. If I allowed myself to continue, wallowing in my own imperfections and beating myself up, I would never have made it over that mountain.

There will always be those who are either better or worse at something than I am. Constantly comparing myself to others could not help me conquer that mountain. I needed to do it my way. To dig deep, seek my own inner strength and find my own way over.

3. Align your mind with your goal.

As I suffered with the running comparison in my head, I realised that I was not serving myself well. I was not mentally aligning with my goal. By focusing on the drama of my suffering, I was pulling myself deeper into drama and not higher up the mountain. By allowing my mind to run amok, I was not accessing my true power. I was not strengthening myself but, rather, dragging myself into weakness.

Therefore, I aligned my mind. My goal was to cross the Pyrenees in a healthy state of body, mind and spirit, and this is where I aligned my mind. I began by visualising myself reaching Roncesvalles in Spain physically fit, mentally strong and with the spirit to continue. I reinforced this vision by practising gratitude. With each step I trudged, my mantra was a drum-like 'Thank! You! Thank! You! Thank! You!' By allowing my mind to be grateful for my body and accessing my indomitable spirit, I aligned with my goal.

4. Ask for help and accept it.

There was a point close to the 10-kilometres mark where I thought I could not continue. I still had another 16 kilometres to go, and all seemed lost. I needed a miracle, and I needed one fast! My help came from an unlikely source, another suffering pilgrim named Brendan. We seemed to lag behind the hundreds of others, and when I asked him if he would like to suffer along with me and walk together, his affirmative reply was instant. By asking for help, I remembered a valuable lesson. Help sometimes comes in unlikely forms, and to reap the benefits I need to be willing to accept it.

Brendan had no superpowers that alleviated our suffering or transported us miraculously over the mountain. What he had was a willingness to walk with a stranger and share of himself as he went. Walking together, we immediately found that our burden lightened. Our perspective of our suffering changed. We were in it together. Together we were strong, and somehow the journey became easier.

5. Plan your descent strategy.

Climbing a mountain means that at some stage there is a descent involved. Many times we focus all our energy on ascending the mountain, conquering it, overcoming it and showing it who is boss, and we forget that we also need to descend. The way you descend a mountain is very different to how you ascend it. You need to embrace different skills, be aware of how the environment has changed and use your body and mind in a new way. By being careless in the descent, you can cause injury and ruin the rest of the journey. Therefore, it is wise to have a sound strategy in place, to know what your options are and when to deploy them.

Often we think descending is plain sailing, but most times it is not. Give yourself time, make adjustments and continue to learn lessons and exercise as much bravery coming down the other side as you did going up.

6. Savour your successes.

Walking over the Pyrenees was a major feat for me. I know thousands accomplish this each year, and, in the scheme of things, this is not a big deal. However, that is not true. By accomplishing what I thought improbable, I now have a new yardstick for conquering my own limitations. I have learnt not to diminish an accomplishment but rather to celebrate it. By allowing myself to savour the sweet taste of success, I know how deep are my reserves of resilience, resourcefulness and perseverance.

If you are climbing a mountain today, I hope these six tips will help strengthen your resolve and bring you courage to continue.

Buen Camino!

Blog Post 3: How Walking the Camino Taught Me Not to Suffer

Date: Tuesday, 30 June 2015, 11:26

This past week, two events occurred with the potential to cause me suffering – if I allowed them to. The first was the much anticipated and welcomed visit of my dear friend, Donna, who I met on the Camino. The second was learning of my uncle's murder in his home in London. The common element of these two events is my attachment to the people involved.

As human beings, we seem to have a strange need to attach ourselves to people, places and things. The Buddha said, 'To be free from suffering, free yourself from attachments.' This seems as futile as trying to leap to the moon from my chair. However, eventually walking 900 kilometres across Spain in the blistering heat and summer thunderstorms opened my understanding to the truth of this teaching.

The Camino, in my experience, is all about the people you meet and the relationships you forge. This includes meeting yourself and building a strong, loving relationship to you. A strange phenomenon occurs along the Camino. Within moments of meeting a total stranger, you create a deep and lasting soul bond. You feel as if you have known this person your whole life and that your souls are irrevocably and intimately intertwined. You experience immense love, compassion, empathy, trust, acceptance and support for them. You might even find yourself wondering why you are doing that, knowing that in daily life you would never be so open to strangers. And yet you cannot seem to help yourself. Likewise, as you fall in love with your new tribe or family, you sense, even from a great distance, who are the people you should avoid at all costs. In the past year, I have tried to understand this phenomenon. I have asked others their opinions and tried to make sense of it, and I cannot. I simply accept it for what it is: me seeing and loving the best in others.

There is a golden rule to walking a successful and happy Camino. Each must go The Way Their Way. This is very difficult when you are creating so many wonderful connections along The Way. You want to stay a while, settle and hold onto the moment, the person and the place. You forge attachments. Then your suffering begins. Perhaps you start walking too fast and injure your feet, shins or hips. Perhaps you say goodbye and wish that you had not. You begin obsessing about where your new friend is, will you see them again, and why did you not connect on Facebook or get their last name. Caught up in your thoughts, you are no longer present with yourself. Reading this, you may think that I am a stalker of sorts, but I assure you this is not the case. This is attachment and Camino suffering in its purest form. Since I form deep connections to others, this was the first type of suffering that I experienced.

There was also my attachment to places. When I arrived at a beautiful town or city, a longing set in. I wanted to settle, noted similarities to other places I loved, wanted the moment to linger longer than necessary. I also noted the suffering of my mind. I was deeply attached to thought patterns, processes, past and non-existent future events. I was suffering in my bad attitudes, in my love for those passed on, in my strongly held beliefs and in my mental drama about my physical pain.

It was when I realised that pain is inevitable but suffering optional that I could start halting my suffering. I learnt that detaching from attachments is a choice. We all have things that we love to hold on to. The question is: Do they bring us joy? Do they bring us freedom? Do we experience our best selves by remaining attached to them? In my experience, the answer is no.

I continue to learn that I need to make strong choices. I need to let go, be it of people, places, thoughts or things. I am by no means saying that I want to live my life not caring about the world around me. I am saying that I am choosing not to hold onto things that should be free. In doing so, I am experiencing more freedom within.

There is much 'truth' in suffering. When we observe the mental and verbal arguments and justifications around our suffering, much of it is true. Yes, the child did not deserve to die so young. Yes, the love of your life should not have beaten you. And, yes, there is no justification for murder. All of this is true. What I have found is that the 'truth' can also take us on a tightly wound downward spiral. Becoming so attached to our way of thinking, we fall into a sinkhole of truth. There is no way out. Sometimes you have to catapult yourself away from your truth by choosing to let it go. This does not mean that your truth is no longer true; it means that you will not allow yourself to suffer any longer by holding on to it so tightly.

Freedom is not free. There is a price to pay for freedom. It is not free. Freedom is the only condition for happiness, but we have to *choose* freedom. We have to make that choice. Nelson Mandela taught us that we could be free in mind, body and soul while being physically imprisoned. This was their choice: letting go of attachments to set themselves free. This can also be our choice.

Why would Donna's visit and my uncle's murder have caused me suffering if I allowed them to? It is simple: I wanted them both to stay. I wanted the pleasure of enjoying Donna's company and my uncle's life for longer. I wanted to create more beautiful memories together, to hold onto a moment, to forge deeper attachments. Donna could have stayed longer – this is true. The person responsible for my uncle's murder committed an evil deed – this is true. I felt sad as my friend departed, and I wished that she lived on this continent. I felt numbed, shocked and utterly helpless by the heinous event that took my uncle from us, and yet I had to make a choice. I had to let go.

Suffering is the consequence of making non-life-affirming choices. While I feel deep emotions about the events of the past week, I am choosing not to suffer through them. I feel the pain, I am grateful for the lessons I continue to learn, but I choose not to surrender my happiness through enslavement to attachments. In the words of Thich Nhat Hanh, 'Letting go gives us freedom, and freedom is the only condition for happiness.'

Buen Camino!

Blog Post 4: Six Simple Actions to Gain Clarity

Date: Tuesday, 7 July 2015, 13:15

Don't you just love that a question mark is an exclamation mark in waiting? It is the same thing expressed differently. It is a HUH? waiting to become YES! We all have experienced times of fear and confusion in our lives. We know what it is like to be in a state of questioning with no clarity in sight. What happens when we become stuck in that state? Speaking from experience, I know how debilitating this can be. We do not necessarily want to become stuck, but the more we question, the more we become drawn into our questioning. Perhaps this is why the question mark has a curved top, like a hook, keeping us hooked into a situation.

So how do we release the hook, stand up straight, gain clarity and move on? I believe that we look for the action that will move us on. We look for our arrow or sign. There always is one. One of the things I loved about the Camino Francés was that The Way was always clearly signposted. The yellow arrow or scallop shell indicates The Way, and pilgrims quickly learn to look for these signs on walls, street corners, lamp posts, obscure stones, etc. You simply follow the signs until you see the next one. Believe me, pilgrims get lost, confusion sets in, you swear at your guidebook and become anxious, but most pilgrims know to go back to the point where they last saw an arrow and continue from there. How easy if life were like this. Perhaps it is.

1. Stick with what you know.

When we are self-aware, we know that we can tap into ourselves when confusion sets in. Some have highly developed intuition; others trust their 'gut' or their 'heart'; while others are very cerebral and rational in confusing times. Use whatever works for you. If your partner is a gut person and you are a head person, stick with your head. Do not add more confusion to the plot.

2. Remember past successes.

Remind yourself of another time you were confused, stuck and lacked clarity. Remember how you overcame in that situation. Savour that past success and remember that if you could do it once you can do it again. We have all overcome obstacles. We have all let go of hooks. Remember and build on the success. It is not always necessary to reinvent the wheel, but it is possible to use past successes as stepping stones.

3. Pay attention.

Confusing situations often seem isolating and lonely. It can feel like no one understands or cares. I know that the Universe conspires to help us and that there are multiple signs showing us the way. Pay attention. Start connecting the dots. Look for further signs. No, it is not luck or coincidence when everything around you seems to be speaking to your situation. In your confused, questioning, stuck state, you are required to be aware and pay attention.

4. Follow the signs, take action.

Awareness is wonderful, but without action it does not bring about clarity or change. To turn a question mark into an exclamation mark, you must act. You can wait for ever for 100-percent certainty and clarity. You can wait until all risks are removed, and you can continue as an awareness junkie, but this does not straighten out that question mark. It does not create YES!

5. Take small steps.

Moving away from uncertainty is frightening. If you have been stuck in that place for a while, there is a certain warmth and comfort there. Be kind to yourself:

take small steps in the direction of clarity. Trust yourself and take it one step at a time. Practise patience and kindness.

Often when we move away from the question we want to leap into the exclamation. This can happen, but be aware that a Eureka moment is not always waiting behind every question. Sometimes we need to let it unfold. We need to continue taking action, creating experience, taking small steps, allowing our questions to straighten out towards clarity.

6. Spend time outside.

Scientific research has shown that we experience less stress and more happiness as we spend time outdoors in nature. I have found that a great way for me to go from HUH? to YES! is walking in the forest near my home. It is in these moments that I can start straightening out that question, gaining clarity, creating my YES! Trust me on this: It really works. After walking 900 kilometres in thirty-four days in all sorts of weather conditions, I know how happy one can become paying attention, following the signs, taking small steps each day and allowing the habit of clarity to form.

Buen Camino!

Blog Post 5: What Walking the Camino Taught Me about Gratitude

Date: Tuesday, 14 July 2015, 16:43

This past Sunday, The German and I went hiking with friends along the Eggeweg hiking trail where we live. This is a beautiful 75-kilometre hike through forest and farmland, which we decided to walk in three parts. Our second phase of the trail we walked in less than ideal conditions. It rained most of the day, with various degrees of hardness. At times it was windy and cold, and there was no sign of sunshine. The trail was muddy and slippery, the forest eerily mysterious, and we were the only hikers.

The conditions for misery were perfect. There were moments when I wondered why we were doing this to ourselves, and then I remembered important lessons in gratitude that were reinforced along the Camino. I remembered that a year ago I was making my way up to Cruz de Ferro and all the events that unfolded at that iron cross. I thought of the three stones I had carried, unsure of their significance, knowing only that three was the correct number to carry. I remembered stepping onto that mound with a fair amount of uncertainty and sending up a silent prayer asking for guidance and clarity. Not only was it a threshold moment for me, it was also a breakthrough moment because, as I stepped off that mound, I knew these three things for sure.

1. Gratitude takes us places.

Many times, life is unclear. We cannot see the forest for the trees. Our fears and insecurities overwhelm us, and we become immobile in our doubts. When we practise gratitude each moment of each day, it takes us places. It gives our life momentum, it brings us to our answers, and it shows us our destination.

The energy of gratitude is not egoistic but rather humble. It helps us create a different perspective of our world. We are not all grateful for the same things because all our life experiences are different. However, whatever you or I are grateful for, we should express that gratitude. I have found that having a gratitude mantra helps. While walking the Camino, it was 'Thank! You! Thank! You!' with each step I took. This was my vehicle, the simple way gratitude took me places. What simple gratitude mantra could you practise today to take you to new places?

2. Gratitude is not a feeling, it's a choice.

Many times we think we should be grateful when we are happy – when the sun is shining, the birds are singing, and all is well with the world. Actually, this is the worst time to practise gratitude as it is based on emotion and not choice. I am not saying that we should not be grateful when we are happy, I am saying that we can choose to be grateful when we are not.

The energy of gratitude is greater than the given circumstance, and, by choosing to align with it, we elevate ourselves above our present circumstances be they happy or not. In which areas of your life will you choose to practise more gratitude today?

3. Gratitude defeats criticism.

We are often our own worst critics. If we made public our self-conversations and self-condemnations, our shame would be complete. Most of us would never treat a dear friend the way we allow our inner critic to treat us, and yet we do.

When we practise gratitude, it defeats criticism. Gratitude closely aligns with the energy of love, joy, harmony and peace, thereby squeezing out the critic, the one who wants to bring us down. This is true not only for our inner selves but also in our relationships with others. When we practise gratitude and appreciation towards others, we become more loving and kind towards others. Can you defeat your inner critic today through gratitude?

In this past year, the lessons in gratitude have continued. It is not always easy. Often I become caught up in the drama within or around me and forget that gratitude is actually my life force. It is the strongest choice I can make each day. Regardless of the circumstances, only for today I will be grateful.

Blog Post 6: Three Quick Tips for Remaining Focused

Date: Tuesday, 21 July 2015, 7:48

Most of us make resolutions coming into a new year. By 3 January, many have broken them. I no longer make resolutions. It seems like an exercise in futility as often I become embroiled in the holiday-season festivities and excitement of entering a fresh, clean new year. However, as my birthday rolls around each year, I am often introspective and reflective of the year that has been and the one that is to come. This is a good time to regain or remain on focus for me.

Today is my birthday, and, yes, I am happy to be 'ageing' into more grace and wisdom. When I reflect on the 365 days that have passed, I can only marvel at the journey I have undertaken. This has been one of the most challenging years of my short life and also one of the most fulfilled, inspired and joyful. Shortly before my last birthday I set some major goals for my life. Actually, this is not fully true. I can say I made some grand statements, and the Universe conspired with me to make them happen.

I have not always remained on point, but, reflecting on my life, I see that in this past year I have been more focused than ever before. What has been different? Looking back, these three practices and habits have enabled me to remain focused with greater consistency.

1. Know your purpose.

The Bible says that, 'He who has no vision perishes,' and I find this to be true. When we lack vision or a sense of purpose, we allow things to drift, forget our direction, and become rudderless.

We each have purpose in life. Even seemingly insignificant parts of our bodies, such as the appendix, have purpose. Horrible horse flies have purpose. This year, I chose to align myself closely to my chosen life purpose and to live on purpose. When doubts and insecurities set in or the sense of purpose diminished, I consciously brought my purpose back into my vision. Even though I cannot see around the next corner does not make the purpose invisible. It is always there, and I need to remain purposeful in thought and deed to maintain focus.

2. Hold fast to your values.

Many people think that their values remain unchanged. From my experience, I do not find this to be the case. When I was younger, I valued different things to what I do now. Where I once valued money, I now value abundance. Where I once valued popularity, I now value deep, lasting relationships. Knowing what I value and how my values affect me each day helps to keep me focused on my chosen purpose in life and keeps me on track when distractions, big and small, come along. When new opportunities arise and old challenges resurface, I perform a quick mental audit to see how they align with my values. If the situation is unaligned with my values, I have learnt to walk away much faster than previously. Knowing what I value enables me to reduce unnecessary clutter in my mind and life. When was the last time you checked in with your values?

3. Practise mindfulness.

Jon Kabat-Zinn has popularised the idea of mindfulness in modern society. Stemming from Buddhist tradition, it is the intentional, accepting and non-judgemental focus of one's attention on the emotions, thoughts and sensations occurring in this present moment. In a society where *mindlessness* seems prevalent – losing my mind, mindless speech, television, violence, etc. – is it not wonderful to take responsibility for your mind in a non-judgemental, accepting manner?

Mindfulness involves not only meditation but all activities in our lives. We can apply it to walking, talking, eating, socialising, loving. Being present in this moment, slowing down, being aware – this has been one of the greatest habits cemented for me this past year by walking the Camino.

To remain focused, I now practise these three steps daily. Knowing my chosen purpose on a deep inner level keeps me from falling out of the boat when the seas become choppy. Being mindful of the moment and present within myself reminds me that this too shall pass and that, in this moment, all is well. Reminding myself constantly of what I value and hold to be true is my yardstick by which I measure everything.

Buen Camino!

PART III

BACK TO THE WAY

'Your Camino only starts when you reach home.' –
Gilles Gans

The in-between story

So there I was, each week, 'happily' reflecting on some of the many lessons I had learnt along The Way, but the truth is I was actually in quite a lot of turmoil. You see, when I wrote the first blog post on my first anniversary I was feeling indomitable. I was in a space of KNOWING my fear but persisting anyway. I felt like 'I had arrived.' I knew where I was going, and I knew how to get there. How wrong was I!

On the evening of 16 June 2015, I participated in a coaching support call with other coaches. The topic was fear, and, as I was feeling quite fearless, I had a lot to share about my own experiences. The conversation progressed onto another topic, and Ann and Courtney began speaking about their 'superpowers'. I was unfamiliar with the topic and asked them to elaborate. They explained to me that they had done various exercises to answer the questions, 'If you were a superhero, what would be your superhero name?' and 'If you were a superhero, what would be your superpower?' I listened to them explaining the process of what they had discovered about themselves and felt quite inadequate.

My thoughts were racing. I was thinking, Oh God, I don't have any superpowers. How the hell do I go about doing this? Besides, I'm so far behind everyone else, all the good superpowers are taken! To be honest, I kind of blended out their voices and fell into a few moments of self-pity and woe. That fearlessness I had felt moments previously evaporated, and I sat like a lump of inadequacy upon my sofa.

In the midst of my crazy thought processes, I heard a very calming voice speak directly to my heart. Spirit said to me, 'Angela, you do not need a superhero name, and you do not need any superpowers. You were named at birth; you already have your superpower.'

And, of course, as I am prone to do, my first reaction was questioning: 'What the friggin' hell?! What does that mean?! How the heck?!' And off my mind went, at a million miles an hour.

Spirit remained calm in the midst of my drama and said, 'Angela, you were named at birth. This is your superhero name, and your name is what you must do. You are an angelic messenger; you are here to help people find their way back to themselves and to help them find healing.'

I don't know about you, but this sounds crazy and overwhelming and too much to bear and did I mention crazy? However, the truth is I knew it to be true. I walked to find what was looking for me, and I thought I had found it, and, in part, I had, but I had not seen the full picture. I had not received the last piece of the beautiful puzzle.

What did I do with this wonderful information? I became insecure, started doubting, and fell into a mini-crisis of sorts. I wondered how the hell do you 'sell' this? How do you package this 'gift' in a way that people want to 'buy' it? I began looking at everything I had created in the past year and found it unworthy. I actually wanted to run away and hide. This felt like too much. I was being required to expose too much of myself to the world. Part of me, the brash, big-mouthed, egocentric know-it-all that I had spent so many years refining, was struggling to give up and allow itself to be buried. 'No!' it yelled, 'You have to protect yourself! You can't be so exposed to the world! And, besides, let's be honest, who the hell do you think you are? Angelic messenger? Oh, come on now, be real!'

I felt quite tormented within myself. This is what I knew to be true within the very core of my being. The past year and a half had been all about awakening myself, about being who I am, about living who I am – about creating a synergy between the two that who I am and what I do are the same. Yet when I heard it expressed so clearly, all those fears, doubts and insecurities shot to the surface.

As I am prone to do, I kept all of these things very close to my heart. I had business concerns in that I had no paying clients, there did not appear to be any on the horizon, and I was feeling like a general failure. The more I tried to do, the further away the results seemed to be. I reached out to my sister on 8 July via Skype, and she was having what I call a Hallelujah Jesus moment. I told her how I was feeling about my revelation and trying to tie it together with my business and the fact that I had no business as I had no clients.

Her messages for me were extremely pertinent. She reminded me that fear is False Evidence Appearing Real. She encouraged me to continue to be an extravagant giver. She reminded me of the high value I place on giving, and she encouraged me to give although I felt like I had nothing of worth or value to give. She said to me, 'Angie, your whole life has been about the unexpected. It is from the unexpected that the most amazing things come forth for you. Expect the unexpected and allow it to happen. Please remember never to despise the days of small beginnings!'

Her words stuck with me the whole day, and I was thinking, Where the friggin' hell is the unexpected supposed to come from? I feel like I live in the boondocks here in Germany. How is the unexpected going to manifest for me here?

When I fall into a fretful place, I have difficulty sleeping, and that night I was trawling Facebook for distraction and entertainment. I saw a post by a friend, Rebekah Scott, author of *The Moorish Whore*, which asked for *hospitaleros* (volunteers) for two weeks in July along the Camino because one of the *hospitaleros* had to cancel due to a family emergency. Rebekah is very involved with various Camino associations and was responsible for staffing some *albergues* with volunteers. My heart skipped a beat, and I immediately sent her a message requesting more details. I did not think I could do two weeks, but if everything fitted together, I would volunteer for a week.

The details were very limited, and, until Rebekah replied, I was in the dark, but my mind immediately flew to the Camino, and I wondered where, when, what could be the possibilities. I eventually went to bed and told the sleepy German, 'Sweetie, I think we're going to Spain.' Her loving reply was, 'Shut up now and sleep.'

Early in the morning, The German shook me awake and asked if I had been mumbling something about Spain. I assured her that I had and that she should prepare herself for the possibility of a trip to Spain. It was early in the evening of the next day that I heard from Rebekah. She filled me in on the details, and we had a Skype call together. I was excited about the possibility of returning to Spain with The German in tow and introducing her to The Way. She was not that keen. She saw this as being 'my thing', but intuitively I put my call with Rebekah on loudspeaker so that she could listen in. Throughout the conversation, I could feel her energy levels changing. As Rebekah spoke of what was required and where I would be stationed, I did not need any time to reconsider or sleep on it. I immediately said, 'Yes, I will come.'

I had committed to arriving in Spain by Friday, 24 July, so I had two weeks to prepare. A few things immediately occurred to me. The 24th of July was the day that I started walking the Camino Finisterre with Donna and Phil. I would be driving back home on 1 August, and this was the day I had arrived home from my pilgrimage the previous year. It felt like Spain had something for me that I needed to receive – I did not know what that was; however, I still heard my sister's voice fresh in my mind so I decided to expect the unexpected.

My greatest motivation was that I simply wanted to go there and to serve with love. I wanted to be a blessing to fellow pilgrims and position myself to love them and serve them as they required. I knew I would be filling some large shoes as I had seen so many wonderful examples of loving *hospitaleros* on my pilgrimage. Additionally, I would be stationed at San Antón, and I have already shared with you how deeply my heart and soul were touched when I stopped briefly there. I felt nervous as I had received no official *hospitalera* training, but Rebekah assured me that everything would be fine. I would be serving with a German pilgrim named Oliver, and he had years of experience. One thing The German and I do very well together is host guests from around the world in our home. Therefore, hospitality is not new to me, so I decided not to fret unnecessarily.

As we drove away from home early in the morning on 23 July, I felt very excited. I knew once again that the Camino was calling me – I just did not know for what purpose. I knew to expect the unexpected because conditions at San Antón would not be easy. I was heading into a week without electricity, hot water, a limited water supply and no Wi-Fi, which all seem to be modern-day accessories for happiness! My heart was also rejoicing because my sweetie had decided to accompany me. She decided to walk a part of the Camino in the Meseta from Burgos during the week as I served, and I was overjoyed that she would get to experience what was my favourite part of the Camino.

The Eighth Letter from San Antón, Spain

From: Angela Barnard,
angela@inspireforlifecoaching.com
To: Dear Friends
Subject: The Camino gives you what you need
Date: Saturday, 25 July 2015, 17:55

Yesterday I arrived in Spain to begin my volunteer stint as a *hospitalera* at the San Antón monastery. It was a long and arduous drive, taking two days, and when we arrived, my fellow *hospitalero* gave me a quick rundown of how everything works. As it was late afternoon, there seemed to be very few pilgrims coming by. A few people stopped and looked at the ruins, but none were interested in staying the night.

Eventually, close to 7 p.m., Oliver announced that he was going for a night out on the town, as it seemed unlikely that we would be hosting any pilgrims. I was enjoying the early evening ambience around the monastery, feeling slightly inadequate. First day on the job and no pilgrims! The German, who stayed with me overnight before beginning her Camino today, suggested that we make ourselves dinner, have a cold shower and retire early to bed to recover from the long drive.

Honestly speaking, there was more to my feelings of inadequacy than I was letting on. I felt that my 'first day on the job' was reflecting what was happening in my life now. Starting my own business has required great fortitude, resilience, patience and business acumen. I would say the skill I lack the most is sales skills. Currently, I have experienced a fair amount of anxiety around client acquisition, and, while I have done everything I am capable of doing, I now await for the seeds to take root, so to speak.

I asked The German if this was going to be a week without pilgrims. Have my business issues followed me to the Camino and is this a further test? I was reassured that the pilgrims would come. 'Don't worry. The ones who want to stay here will come when they are ready.' After hearing this, I felt a strong sense and reminder just to be. Not to worry about doing, and making, and planning, and busy-ness, but just to be. I realised that if not one pilgrim decided to stay over this coming week I am still exactly where I need to be. I took a moment to breathe deeply, to recommit to just being and to enjoy the moment.

Through the gorgeous gateway came a local man on a bike looking for Oliver. Even with poor Spanish I understood that he lives locally, hails originally from Madrid and likes to pop into the *albergue* and visit with the volunteers and pilgrims. I mentioned that there were no pilgrims but offered him a glass of wine. We had just poured a glass when three travel-weary pilgrims ambled through the gigantic stone entrance. 'We are not too late are we? Do you still have beds available for us?' they asked, concerned.

I quickly evaluated them and joked that as long as they were not the drunken and disorderly types they were welcome to stay. They seemed incredulous that they were the first guests and could not understand why the *albergue* was not full. After I showed them to their beds and discussed dinnertime with them, I left them to freshen up and perform their pilgrim ablutions. We were just about to start cooking when another two bedraggled pilgrims came in, dragging old-fashioned wooden carts behind them. They too were surprised that there was space available.

It was time to spring into action and start preparing a meal for seven people by candlelight. The German and I worked efficiently in unity, and in no time all the pilgrims had freshened up under the cold shower and dinner was on the table. At first I wondered if we should not try to track down Oliver, but then I realised that all was well; this was a small challenge for me to deal with. I felt so blessed with my first pilgrim dinner with my first pilgrims. As we started eating, I shared my joy with them, and it was a delightful evening of fellowship, friendship, great food and some fine guitar-playing and singing. The evening filled with love and laughter as people shared their stories, challenges and triumphs. We each recognised ourselves in one another and simply delighted in being.

In typical Camino fashion, the first group of three had met only that day. They were the awesome, soulful Austin from the USA, newly graduated Anastasia from Germany and a young school graduate named Dom from Lithuania, who had walked 80 kilometres the previous day. The second couple were Russ from England and his German partner, Sylvia. They have been walking since April, have completed two Caminos this year and are currently walking back to Frankfurt in Germany.

I came to Spain with the intention to offer service through love. I am cognisant of the incredible love I received from numerous angels as I walked last year, and I hope to give back a small piece of what I received. Before I fell asleep, I realised it is true: the Camino does give us what we need. The five people who arrived last night were the perfect match for my first day on the job. During the day, other people had popped in, and, in my 'neediness' to have pilgrims, I wanted to convince them to stay, but they were not the right fit for me.

I was in need of reassurance that if I plant the right seeds in my business they will grow, that the people I am meant to work with will come and that I will be able to serve through love in my work. How often do we pursue relationships in life or business that we know we should not? We come from a certain place of neediness or wanting something, and often these relationships are fraught with stress and strife. There is not a natural ease, a state of being where both parties mutually benefit from the relationship.

So that was my first day, and, already, the Camino has provided me with a powerful lesson and reminder: Angela, allow yourself to be. Don't try to force something to happen because you are desperate (or think you are!) or in a place of neediness. Trust that if you have planted the seeds and continue to nurture them that in their season they shall flourish and produce a good harvest. All is well right now, although I may not always see that right now.

Perhaps this is the only experience I came to Spain to create, perhaps not. I continue to water the seeds of intention to serve with love each day.

The Ninth Letter from San Antón, Spain

From: Angela Barnard,
angela@inspireforlifecoaching.com
To: Dear Friends
Subject: The joy of extravagant giving and receiving
Date: Sunday, 26 June 2015, 14:58

Last weekend I was chatting with friends about giving and receiving. We all noted how we behave in social situations. When invited to a dinner party, we all take a small – or sometimes not so small – gift for the host. When invited out for coffee, we quickly jump in attempting to pay the bill. We noted how more and more we are becoming a bartering society. You give me this, therefore I will give you that.

In my opinion, it takes the joy out of giving. In the name of social conventions or politeness, we do not want to lose face and need to keep up with others at all costs. Lately I have been asking myself critical questions around the topic of giving and receiving. I know that I am an extravagant giver, but I am not such an extravagant receiver. Do I see myself as weak or vulnerable if I am on the receiving end? Perhaps I feel I am abdicating power by being the receiver.

As I volunteer here at San Antón, I set the intention each day that just for today I will serve with love. I will give generously, and I will be a blessing to others. These are noble intentions to have, right? Yesterday afternoon, things were once again slow, and no pilgrims were popping into the ruins. I decided to walk towards the road and look for some action, and, as I approached the front gate, I saw a lone pilgrim slightly following the curvature of the road to come towards San Antón.

I asked the man, James, if he intended to stay with us and if he would like to view the facility. Together we made our way towards the entrance, and I allowed him that breathless moment when he first viewed the ruins and imbibed the view for the first time. Before he left this morning he said to me that I had 'lured him in with charm', making me sound like a Camino siren of sorts. What I did not know was that I needed to be on the receiving end of a powerful message.

Yesterday was the feast day of St James, and Ovidio Campo Fernandez, the patron of San Antón, came with his family to celebrate the feast day with the pilgrims in the *albergue*. They had prepared for us a delicious meal, and, once again, the dinner table lit up with generous laughter, love, food and fellowship. As dinner progressed, I learnt a little more about James, a cinematographer from London who made a rather spontaneous decision to walk the Camino, which he is walking to raise money for charity in loving memory of his brother.

For a long time, James has been feeling that there is something that he must do: make a film about people undergoing major life changes and turning things around for themselves. He took out a few bank loans to finance the project, and next year he would like to return to the Camino to record the pilgrims' wonderful stories. James told me that he doesn't know if this project will succeed or fail, if he will fall into debt and need to take jobs he hates, but what he is learning is that the more he gives, gives and gives, the more he receives. He said this is a law of the Universe that regardless of what he gives or to whom it always comes back many fold.

As he spoke, his energy became electric. I could see that he has previously and is currently experiencing the joy of extravagant giving. What he did not know was that he was also giving to me. He was bolstering my spirit and reminding me of wisdom I hold as true. I know that when I give from a place of pure love without expectation, judgement or neediness that I, as the giver, experience absolute joy. I do not feel an attachment to the outcome, it is as if that which I am giving is simply passing through or over me onto the next person, and I am simply a conduit. By not being an extravagant receiver, I disempower another from being an extravagant giver.

Often our society tells us the exact opposite. The lie is that there must be something in it for us, otherwise others will take advantage of us and take us for granted. It is even said that no good deed goes unpunished. Is this not just ridiculous? It is not easy to set aside these messages, to set aside our gigantic egos and simply allow extravagant giving. I also realise that when we do not allow extravagant receiving we are blocking the flow of all the wonderful things that can come to us.

Being an extravagant giver does not mean being flashy, flamboyant or excessive. This is how most people would define extravagance. For me it means not limiting the flow, being open to all possibilities – not restraining them but simply allowing. This always starts with my attitude. When I restrain my attitudes and intentions, my giving and receiving are also restrained.

These were some powerful lessons to remember. In fact, I need to remember them each day if I want to live a joyous life. Thank you, James, for walking into my life and adding some flavour to the wisdom I already know to be true.

The Tenth Letter from San Antón, Spain

From: Angela Barnard,
angela@inspireforlifecoaching.com
To: Dear Friends
Subject: Finding harmony through the five elements
Date: Monday, 27 July 2015, 18:46

Have you ever experienced a moment so pure that it could be a dream, and, when you awaken, you are overjoyed to discover that it is not? Yesterday at San Antón I experienced two such moments. I had the pleasure of an unexpected but most welcome visit from Rebekah Scott, who lives in Moratinos. Previously I had spoken with her only on Skype and Facebook, and it was really a delight to meet face to face. Our conversation was both random and intense.

Rebekah shared with me how much she loves the air energy of San Antón. There is no roof on this ruin, and the limitlessness of sky and air now abound through the crumbling façade. It leaves one feeling awed. One experiences new perspectives in a house of

God that has no roof as a barrier to the elements or to the Almighty.

I shared with Rebekah some thoughts and concerns I had about being a *hospitalera*. She reminded me that my main 'element' is earth, which is grounded and still. Oliver is very air-dominant, and, strangely enough, there have been times I have felt breathless around him, like he takes up all the air in the room. Rebekah reminded me of how air, fire, water and earth all exist together, with different forms and functions, but ultimately in harmony. It was a lovely visit, and, as Rebekah left, she encouraged me to continue listening for the things I need to hear and to allow myself to be.

In the early evening, a Spanish couple walked in to view San Antón. I was chatting to a pilgrim and paid them little attention until we became aware of the music. The lady was sitting on a bench facing the main entrance and singing. It was heavenly. The acoustics of the building picked up her voice, and it filled the space like an arena. I slowly made my way over to her and sat next to her on the bench. I felt drawn to be there.

She seemed a little put off by my presence, but I asked if I might sit with her as she sang. She overcame her stage fright, or the annoyance of having me in her space, and began to sing, this time 'Ave Maria'. In the moment she sang, I felt the gravitational pull of the Earth pulling me in, my eyes closed, my ears opened, and I felt the air and heard the water. Her voice was so melodious, like a clear brook tinkling over a rocky outcrop. As she sang, the air picked up her voice and breathed it back over my body. I was aware that I was crying but felt helpless to wipe away the tears or respond in any other way but allow the love of that moment to love me.

As she stopped singing, I turned to her and whispered, 'Gracias señora.' She was surprised at my tears and told me not to cry, which made me cry more, and she took my face in her hands and gently wiped my tears away with her thumbs. I was not crying in sadness or mourning, but my body was simply responding to the moment of bliss as I allowed the earth, the air and the sound of water in the melody to remind me of the harmony and perfection of each moment.

Much later, in the evening, the half-moon showered San Antón with her light, and I asked the three manly young men from New Zealand and Australia if one of them would accompany me outside. I simply had to experience the power of the moon shining into San Antón from a different perspective and did not want to do it alone. Sam, my new Kiwi friend, who had walked all the way from London with his brother Dave, said he would join me.

We left the premises and walked east, looking back at San Antón through the poplar trees, and then we headed west under the arch towards Castrojeriz. I really liked Sam. In our brief time together we had some profound conversations with one another, and I found his passion for the Camino infectious and inspiring. This was his second Camino, and he had somehow convinced three other people to walk The Way. He is quite the salesman!

We walked slowly down the road and paused briefly to look back and enjoy San Antón in the moonlight. Both of us loved the way the moon shone upon San Antón, and we imagined what this complex must have been like in its prime. We imagined people coming from all over Europe to receive healing there and imagined ourselves walking under the gigantic arches into the church.

The moon drew in our gazes, and we witnessed the most beautiful sight. In the distance were the low-lying hills of the Meseta. The moon hung just above the horizon, in the middle ground stood a lone poplar tree bathed in moonlight, and directly in the foreground two poplar trees had sagged towards one another, forming a perfect archway as if to imitate San Antón. Both Sam and I were speechless. Nature had created her own cathedral, and we stood at the doorway, so to speak, looking in.

I loved the synchronicity of the moment where Eastern and Western philosophy met and the element of wood entered my day. I was finding harmony through the five elements. Is life not wonderful? Things that can be perceived as mundane actually hold much wisdom if we allow ourselves to hear while listening, to see when looking and to know while being.

The Eleventh Letter from San Antón, Spain

From: Angela Barnard,
angela@inspireforlifecoaching.com
To: Dear Friends
Subject: Love stories from the Camino
Date: Tuesday, 28 July 2015, 12:09

Camino love stories fascinate me. Last year as I walked I heard epic tales of people who had fallen in love along the Camino. I wondered where they found the energy for romance or to put their best foot forward, so to speak. Nevertheless, as we say, the Camino gives us what we need, so who am I to argue? I can understand why people could fall in love even amongst the pain and suffering of a long pilgrimage. Those who have walked understand the magical presence of love, kindness, compassion and all those good things found along the Way.

At the start of this year, I set the intention to make 2015 the most loving year of my life. I have decided that I want to experience more love and give more love than previously in my life. Yesterday, I personally experienced three different love stories at San Antón that I would like to share with you now.

As you know, coming here as a *hospitalera* was unplanned and unexpected. In my relationship with The German, I am the one who will dash off into the unknown without a firm plan, so when I started speaking rather airily about volunteering and demanding immediate and unconditional support, this did not go down too well. At first, she did not want to accompany me, because this is 'my thing', but after speaking to Rebekah she had a change of heart. We decided that I would serve and she would walk.

Yesterday morning, after cleaning the *albergue*, I walked to the street to drop off the garbage. Coming down the road, I saw a familiar face. Sweetie had arrived. It was much earlier than expected, and obviously she had changed her plans, but I felt overjoyed to see her. Not everyone has a partner that supports his or her decisions or passions. Not everyone has a partner who believes in them and allows them to be their imperfect, perfect selves. I do, and I am reminded why I love this soul and how incredibly blessed I am to have her in my life.

Diana had a certain euphoria about her, and, although it was early in the second morning of her brief Camino, I could sense that already the spirit of the Camino was with her. She did not want to consume too much of my space or interfere with what

I needed to do at San Antón, and, after a brief coffee, I sent her and her fellow pilgrims on their way with much love.

In the late morning, a French Polynesian pilgrim walked into San Antón. I had been on the road earlier and had seen her coming from a distance, and the thought entered my mind, 'She's coming to you.' As she rested on a bench, I greeted her, and she engaged me in conversation. We spoke randomly about The Way, and she spoke of the weight we carry in our packs. I said to her that sometimes the thoughts we carry are heavier than any weight in a bag, and she began to cry. She apologised profusely for crying and said that she did not know why she was crying. A fountain of words and tears burst forth, and she repeatedly apologised for her behaviour and for wasting my time. She told me that she felt compelled to stop at San Antón and could not understand why she could not stop speaking to me.

My heart filled with the fullness of compassionate love for her, and I knew that I was there for the sole purpose of sharing love with her. She shared her life dream with me, and I asked her when was the last time she felt truly happy. Through weeping tears, she replied, 'This morning, as I walked along the path and saw the strange colours of The Way, I was filled with complete happiness.'

She felt her confession was stupid, insignificant, and wept further, but I only loved her more. I remembered how many tears I cried in absolute joy along The Way. Feeling oneness and love for all that is and all that can be and being unable to prevent myself from being happy. I encouraged her to allow herself to be one with all that is and all that wants to be. I encouraged her to allow the joy and love that is hers to come to her. With insufficient words, I simply loved.

Months ago, I fell in love on one of the Camino Facebook forums. His name was Ibrahim Çelebi from Istanbul, and I seemed incapable of preventing myself from loving him. For an inexplicable reason, he entered my heart, and I simply loved my online friend. As he prepared for his Camino, he asked me many questions, and each time I answered I felt so much excitement and love for what he was about to do.

One afternoon, I received a random message from him. 'Angie,' he wrote, 'When I get to Cruz de Ferro, I am going to pray for you.' This message struck me like a bolt of lightning, and I asked him why he wrote that. He explained that I was on his mind and that he needed to tell me of his intention. Little did he know that I was having a moment of doubt about the very things I had laid down under the Iron Cross. I sent him a chapter from this book where I wrote about the experience, and I felt grateful that the Universe was using my friend in Istanbul to remind me not to be afraid, that all was well.

As I sat outside San Antón yesterday afternoon, enjoying the shade of the poplar trees, I saw a face I knew from Facebook walking towards me. My friend had arrived. Ibrahim had walked 37 kilometres from Burgos to stay overnight in San Antón and meet me face to face. As we fell into each other's arms, we cried and laughed with joy. I asked him how he was, and he burst out, 'I am overwhelmed with gratitude and grace. Every day I die a little on the Camino and come alive again. This place is crazy!'

Last night, my friend and I took crazy selfies, laughed together and shared our hearts with one another. I do not go around telling strange people that I love them, but under the moonlight of San Antón I told my friend, who is not strange, that he has been in my heart since we met. He said the same is true for him. I cannot explain this love, do not need to, I simply cherish it as it is.

The challenge I will leave here with when I return home on Saturday is to continue making 2015 the year of love. Yesterday reminded me that it is not the Camino that makes me loving but the choices I make. I was created in love, I am a part of love, and therefore I must give love. This is not selective, but it is to all people, loved ones, strangers and friends. How blessed am I to have almost 7 billion possibilities to love.

The Twelfth Letter from San Antón, Spain

From: Angela Barnard,
angela@inspireforlifecoaching.com
To: Dear Friends
Subject: I promise I won't bite
Date: Wednesday, 29 July 2015, 10:27

If all insects, reptiles, mammals, all of God's creatures, took the sworn oath, 'I promise I won't bite,' we would surely experience utopia here on Earth. In fact, I am sure the beastly spider that bit me on Sunday evening had taken the oath but then fell into sin and went against its word. If *hospitaleras* entering into service take the oath, why not all of God's creatures along the way? Or was I the only one that got the memo? So, yes, I am having a hissy fit, I am being dramatic, but what the hell when I'm an unwilling blood donor to the *Arachnid* species. Bladdy hell, I can throw as many hissy fits as I like! And, yes, I do know that nobody got the memo, that I'm giving an Oscar-winning performance, but when a tree falls in a forest with no observers, it has still fallen! 'And I'd like to thank my mother and my father and that little arachnid one Sunday evening ... '

So, yes, most likely an itsy-bitsy, teeny-weeny Spanish-speaking spider has me feeling like crap, experiencing shooting pains down my leg, extreme nausea, fever-like symptoms and a headache. I don't do personal disease too well at the best of times, and certainly not in a foreign country without creature comforts.

I left the doctor's office frustrated and irritated. I couldn't understand how a topical cream would help my internal body. I sat on a bench outside his office and was immediately approached by a geriatric pervert. I did not know he was one until he started squeezing my arms and touching my breasts. I spent a good few moments swatting away his wandering hands and bellowing, 'No, señor!' I remembered that last year this pervert had also molested my friend Donna, and I was determined to send him packing. I can change my body language to Super Evil Bitch in milliseconds, and he soon scampered away from me.

Feeling ill and grumpy, I drove back to San Antón. Pilgrims along the way simply irritated the crap out of me. I was unamused by the gangs walking spread out across the road, all immersed in their mobile phones, or the cyclists who encroached onto my side of the road. I realised that continued grumpiness coupled with illness was not going to bring me happiness or make me a blessing to the pilgrims passing by. I decided to call upon the healing powers of San Antón, to speak to my body and bring healing energy into the parts that felt less than optimal.

I know that when I am suffering and miserable others are probably experiencing worse things than I am. So I decided to peel some fresh oranges, sit outside, and offer some refreshments to pilgrims as they passed. I was amazed at how many people 'had no time' or 'didn't like oranges' or simply needed to 'move on'. Many treated me with suspicion as if I would bite, and I felt like erecting a sign saying, 'I promise I won't bite.'

For those who took the time to stop and grab a piece of fresh orange, we had wonderful moments of connection. A Dutch couple asked me why I was doing this, and I confessed that I had been feeling miserable and realised that there were others suffering more than me. Being very narcissistic with my suffering is quite boring, and serving others reminds me that all is well and that I am blessed, even if I want to have a hissy fit of drama. It did not matter that pilgrims were rushing by or were weighted down by their burdens, I just needed to be there to give those who wanted slices of oranges. Not all of the oranges were eaten on the road. I gave the last pieces to a delightful Italian couple who stopped in at San Antón. We shared a few moments of broken English conversation, and then they continued on their way.

Today, I am once again sitting on the road handing out oranges. Again, the pilgrims are doing what pilgrims do: rushing, ambling, suffering, chatting, freewheeling. I've had powerful and loving conversations with Andrea from North Carolina and Lee from Taiwan, and with Hungarian, German, French and Austrian women. Nicola, a South African living in Qatar, has just shared my water, chair and oranges, and it was a pure delight of sharing home-grown humour and Camino love. On the days when I feel grumpy, ill or out of sorts, it is wonderful to remember that the choice not to bite back is my pathway to happiness and joy.

The Thirteenth Letter from San Antón, Spain

From: Angela Barnard,
angela@inspireforlifecoaching.com
To: Dear Friends
Subject: Tolerance, truth, trust, turmoil
Date: Thursday, 30 July 2015, 17:25

All around San Antón within the architecture we can see the Tau cross in prominent display. This is a T-shaped cross where all three ends are expanded. Often in the little window portals four Tau crosses are clustered together in an interesting design. As I've been gazing on these shapes this past week they seem to symbolise four topics I've been grappling with, namely turmoil, tolerance, truth and trust.

Here's the thing, there's over seven billion of us here on this planet, and from the number of armed conflicts currently on Earth, we can see that we have not found a way to coexist peacefully with one another. This is no different for pilgrims on The Way. With so many people living in close proximity to one another, it's not unlikely that at some stage they piss one another off. However, how do we manage ourselves in order to have a peaceful coexistence?

We are now in a time of such great political correctness that the smallest thing seems to create great offence. Without taking things to the extreme, I sometimes find myself experiencing turmoil within because I just don't like how another person is behaving and yet in the quest to be tolerant I may go against my own personal truth.

I've found myself in turmoil this week being around pilgrims who smoke marijuana habitually. Is this a bad thing? I don't believe so as I myself have smoked weed in my life. However, I do realise that this is a sore spot for me as my eldest sister Jenny was a severe addict for many years. This addiction brought much trauma into her life and our family, and I have a really hard time dealing with the habitual consumption of drugs, even soft ones such as marijuana. I notice that I become incredibly tense and just cannot relax. Can I remove myself from the situation? Yes, I can, but then I fret about the consequence to that person and those around them. Is that my responsibility? No, it's not, but I am aware that I'm balancing all these emotions in the hopes of finding an inner equilibrium I can live with.

What happens when personal choice intersects with tolerance and conflict arises? How to show love and tolerance and live in truth with another person when their actions are not aligned with who you are, and still trust that all will be well? I honestly don't know the answer to this question, but here are some of my rambling thoughts on these topics.

I am not sure that absolute freedom exists, yet I know that when we practise perfect love we experience absolute freedom. On the Camino, where thousands walk together each year, we learn to walk in love, to respect one another and to allow each other to be. In fact, we become more tolerant.

A few days ago, I saw that a famous friend of mine deleted a fan from his Facebook page. The fan commented on him being a 'FAG' because he was partying with some gay friends. My friend, who is not gay, mentioned that he will not tolerate haters on his page and deleted the fan. This led me to think about tolerance, and a scenario developed in my mind. What if my friend left the hater on his page, openly advocated gay rights, continued to party with his friends, showed that there is nothing to be afraid of. Would he win the hater over? There is a strong possibility that this would happen and an equally strong possibility that it would not. I wrote on his wall: 'Dear boy, OF COURSE YOU ARE A FAG! A Fabulous All-round Guy! What's wrong with that? Just like I'm a Fabulous All-round Girl! Welcome to my world.' If only becoming more tolerant were so flippant, frivolous and easy.

The topic of tolerance is interesting as we often tolerate others with long suffering. Alternatively, we also seem to be more intolerant as a society where, in a world of addictive likes, should someone be a disliker they are banished eternally from our small worlds. What happens when we cannot tolerate a person's behaviour based on our own morals or beliefs? Do we walk away? Do we apply love and forbearance? Do we try to influence the situation and change the behaviour? What role does absolute freedom then have?

What if our personal truth is in exact opposition to what we see around us? Each of us can justify our beliefs. We have thought about them long enough; therefore, they are now beliefs. But where is the line, and what happens when it is crossed? What is the balance between loving kindness, perfect love and not tolerating a fellow pilgrim's behaviour based on my own truth?

The greatest lesson I learnt as I walked my Camino is that I must live my own truth. At times, I have been in conflict with my own truth. At other times, those around me have been conflicted by my truth. What does it mean to be in complete acceptance and love of myself, experiencing peace and yet causing my fellow human to stumble because my truth is intolerable to them? What is the win-win situation for all?

I think we will always experience some form of turmoil in our lives, be it internal or caused by external events. I think the answer lays somewhere in this truth – I am not responsible for how another person chooses to behave. If that behaviour is affecting me directly then I can choose to deal with it appropriately. I do not have to tolerate any shit from others that goes against my personal values. This also means I need to look at what I tolerate from myself that is not always in my best interests. At the end of the day, we can live in hope that all of us on this pathway of life are trying the best we can at any given moment. Oftentimes, the things we get our knickers in a knot about will not be important a few days later, let alone in a year's time.

The Fourteenth Letter from Somewhere on the German Autobahn

From: Angela Barnard,
angela@inspireforlifecoaching.com
To: Dear Friends
Subject: Ten little words to sum it all up
Date: Sunday, 2 August 2015, 00:45

Darlings,

We departed San Antón shortly before 5:30 a.m. yesterday morning and have been in transit for over eighteen hours. Both The German and I are travel weary and exhausted, and, in an attempt to remain awake, The German posed a thought-provoking question. She wants me quickly to give ten adjectives that best describe my time at San Antón and to then elaborate on them. Seriously? Must I be profound and articulate now when all I want is to recline in my seat and snore?! There really is no rest for the righteous! But, oh wait, I can talk about my favourite topic: The Camino! So let's see.

The first word is 'exhilarating'. Why was it exhilarating? Normally when you go on a journey you travel somewhere, see and experience new things. I went on a journey, but I remained stationary. I stood at the side of the road, and everything I needed to see or experience came to me. I had no control over how it would unfold, I simply had to be there. I had to do what felt right in my heart, for example stand outside San Antón and give people orange slices if they wanted them.

Even cleaning the toilet each day was exhilarating. (Oh God, what am I saying?!) I simply had to be ready, willing and able. There was nothing else for me to do. I feel as if I did nothing, and yet I did absolutely everything, and that was quite exhilarating. I was on the Camino without actually walking, and yet I walked many, many miles with all the people who walked into San Antón, to visit, sit, eat lunch, snap a photograph or stay for the night. It was exhilarating to have so many people share countless wonderful stories with me and to become a part of their story, even for a fleeting moment.

The second word is 'emotional'. It was emotional, probably for the same reasons that it was exhilarating. I think it had a lot to do with me simply being present in the moment and allowing myself to be in the service of other people. When people stopped, I was compelled to listen to their stories, and when asked to share a story, I realised how present the Camino was for me. It wasn't something that happened last year in my life. It's something that's continuing. I realised how every lesson I learnt is continuing to expand and teach me. In this, I see myself evolving and growing.

The third word is 'challenging'. It is challenging to live and work with a stranger for seven days and to be in a place of humility and service. It is challenging to attempt to anticipate the needs of other people. The heat, spider bite, and resulting illness were extremely challenging. Having to make choices each day that upheld my joy and happiness was challenging because, as you know, life is not always a joyful and happy experience.

Not being able to speak Spanish or French or Polish or Hungarian or Bulgarian or Dutch was challenging, and I lost many great opportunities to connect with pilgrims because of my limited language prowess. It was challenging to drive to Spain, and, at the start of the journey with The German, it was very stressful. Today has been a challenge. It's been a long day; we've been on the road now for eighteen hours and still have another two hours before we are home. The greatest challenge of all was setting my ego aside, but I think for the most part that I mastered this.

The fourth word is 'exhausting'. Most days I awoke at six to prepare breakfast for those pilgrims who wanted it. After all the pilgrims left, the door to San Antón remained open, and people began entering the historical facility to visit. This required our attention, and, in the midst of curious visitors, we also had to clean the *albergue*. It's not a gigantic place, but it does take effort and work. We experienced a heat wave, and the temperature rose to 38 degrees Celsius. This in itself is exhausting and takes it out of you. Strangely enough, I don't recall having time for myself because I always had people around me. Whether I was standing on the road or sitting outside, I always went looking for people. I didn't just sit inside San Antón and wait for them to come to me.

What was additionally exhausting was that Oliver was not always there. I don't mean physically but, rather, emotionally. He had been at San Antón for over a month already and was exhausted, so there were times when he simply checked out. Perhaps I overcompensated for this and made myself too available to others, which also drained my energy. Getting to bed after midnight and waking up early was like having a full day at work. This drive home is also exhausting. But, as much as these things were exhausting, they were exhilarating, like perfectly concentric circles that overlap and complement each other.

Let's not forget 'humbling'. It was humbling to be in service of other people, to place their needs before my own. To clean up after others, acting like a Doris with a mop and washing toilets is definitely not my strength, but I served in love. I felt a lot of love as I was mopping and slopping, but The German should not expect a miraculous transformation of house-cleaning from me because that ain't gonna happen!

It was humbling to hold a space for pilgrims to express themselves and be themselves, to listen to their stories of struggle and transformation, to acknowledge that we have the same struggles, hopes, dreams, burdens, aspirations and desires because we all are one. It was humbling to see how others responded to the best within me. Having the opportunity to volunteer was very humbling. I don't know why this opportunity arose a year before I planned it, but it was definitely meant to be.

The sixth word is 'fun'. It was a lot of fun to do this. It was great to be off the grid and not constantly attached to my phone. It was so much fun to be out of the office and experience a new perspective on life. It was a lot of fun to meet people from all over the world: Taiwan, Bulgaria, Hungary, America, Mexico, Qatar, Turkey, Australia, New Zealand and South Africa to mention a few. The whole world quite literally came to my doorstep. I didn't go anywhere, I just stood there waiting, and that was fun.

A lot of nonsense was spoken at the communal dinners each evening. It was hilarious to listen to and remember the suffering of the pilgrims. Hearing people find perspective on life as they walk and then laugh about it was a lot of fun. Meeting Rebekah was fun as was driving into Castrojeriz each day for a hot shower and to observe what was happening in that little village. It was even funny to be molested by the same geriatric pervert who had molested Donna last year. For me, anything that interrupts the mundane routine in life can be fun, and this past week did just that.

The seventh word is 'real'. Being at San Antón felt very real for me because it brought everything back into perspective. My world slowed down, and I remembered not to worry about the things that I tend to worry about. It was as if I could peer beyond the illusions of my own life. I could see through the bullshit and nonsense and condense my life into only those things that have meaning to me.

I remembered again that life is very simple and not to overcomplicate it. This is my greatest responsibility: to keep life simple and to seek joy each day. That felt very real to me. I think a lot of the stuff that we experience or make important is quite meaningless in the greater scheme of things, and I was reminded of that again. Being so close to nature, experiencing the beauty of the waxing moon, sitting each night among the elements, with the whispering wind, twinkling stars and bright moon felt very real to me. If this past week of my life were a fantasy, it felt like a very good fantasy. It was simple, but it was real.

The eighth word is 'centring'. I went to Spain with questions, very aware of the symbolism of arriving on the same day that I began the Camino Finisterre and of returning home after my Camino was completed.

As with the call to walk the Camino, I did not know what I needed to hear, learn or find, and yet, each day, I heard, learnt and found something life-affirming that reaffirmed all that I've been learning and experiencing this past year. I was centred once again in the truths I hold dear about service, giving, receiving, allowing and being. These have been central themes in my life lately, as have lessons on joy, happiness and what it means to make strong choices in my life every single day.

It was centring for me to simply be. It was a week of having absolutely no concerns in the world. Is this not how life could be each day without all the nonsense we create for ourselves? It was centring for the same reasons that it was real for me. This week at San Antón brought me back to myself – not that I had gone anywhere, but it just grounded and centred me once more. San Antón is an energetically powerful place and yet simultaneously soothing. I experienced the elements very strongly while I was there, and this grounded me and centred me once more.

The ninth word is 'inspirational'. In this past week, I learnt and relearnt so many lessons. I learnt again to simply be. I was reminded that I don't have to make or try and force things to happen. I simply need to be and allow. That was the first lesson from last Friday when we arrived. Then I was reminded of the joy of extravagant giving and receiving, what it means to receive and what it means to allow myself to receive.

The other day, I had left my chair outside San Antón and returned to fetch it. Three female pilgrims were sitting on the wall of the adjacent canal, and we struck up a conversation. Two heralded from Austria, and the other was German. One of the Austrian women told me the following story about learning to receive as she walked.

She was walking, and suffering because her bag was far too heavy for her, and her thoughts were adding to her load. A beautiful Korean family, comprising parents and their two small children, passed her. The father saw how she was suffering with her bag and said to her, 'I must take your bag. Please let me carry it for you.' She did not want to release her bag to him as she felt he had his own problems carrying his own load and that of his children. But he insisted and would not take no for an answer.

He told her that when he saw her struggles with her backpack he was reminded of his first days in the army. As young soldiers, he and his company had to complete a twenty-four-hour endurance hike in dreadful conditions. His pack weighed over 36 kilograms, and, after hiking in treacherous conditions without pause, his feet were covered in gigantic blisters and his back felt broken. When he saw how his fellow pilgrim was walking, she reminded him of how he had suffered throughout that day and night. He said she carried her body the same way he had, and he could see that her thoughts were also weighing her down. He told her that he knew how it was to suffer like that and that now he had the strength of body and mind to carry much more weight without suffering. He beseeched her once more to give him her pack. Without further argument, she handed him her heavy load, and he carried it the rest of the day.

She said to me, 'I had to learn to receive from somebody else. I had to learn to allow someone else to give to me.' This was a very powerful lesson for that woman and reminded me of the same lesson I had learnt from James Light when he visited San Antón.

It was inspirational because I realised that the more I allow myself to inhabit my name and the gift of helping others find their way back to themselves, the more joy I experience. When I allow this gift to operate in my life, it brings joy and healing to myself and to others. Without having a gigantic ego, I find this inspirational because it's about aligning with whom I am choosing to be.

It's inspirational to me that The German came with me and experienced her own little Camino. While her experience was different to mine, it was hers, and this is inspiring to me. I find it inspirational that she would step out of her life, travel with me and do crazy things because I asked her to. Thank you sweetheart.

Finally, the last word is 'repeatable'. Why is this repeatable? I loved everything about being a *hospitalera* and having the ability to serve and love others as they walked on The Way. I have a great love for other pilgrims, which I don't quite understand. And I realise it is actually not necessary to understand it – it's simply how it is. I know that at some stage in my life I will own an *albergue* with The German, and together we will be in a position to serve other pilgrims.

Can I imagine myself returning to San Antón to serve? Yes, I can. Was it unbearable to live with a limited water supply, without hot water, electricity and the amenities of everyday life? Can I live without these things? Yes. I don't need any of this stuff to be happy. Was having no Wi-Fi so critical? Do you know that there were people who chose not to stay at San Antón not because there was no hot water or electricity but because there was no Wi-Fi? It was great that I had a car this past week, as it added a different dimension of ease, with which I could do things, but even if I had to walk or cycle I could still imagine myself repeating this experience.

What I appreciated about San Antón was the intimacy of the *albergue* and the ruin. This created a sense of intimacy for the group of pilgrims who stayed each night. There was not one night that I found a pilgrim unbearable or that anyone stayed who bought disharmony to the group through chaos within their own life. I was blessed each day by the people who came – be it to look, take photographs, visit a historical monument or sleep over.

This is what makes San Antón so special compared to other *albergues*. As it is a monument with great historical value and such incredible energy, people don't only come there with the intention of sleeping over. They also come wanting to learn more about the history and to soak up the San Antón energy. There are also those who don't even realise that San Antón is there and simply walk under the giant arch overhanging the road and continue on their way. San Antón is a *donativo albergue*, meaning that pilgrims can donate whatever they want to stay there. This was a valuable experience for me, as I had to put aside my thoughts about what people could or should donate. San Antón offers pilgrims the freedom to be who they are; the rest is inconsequential.

These are my ten powerful little words summing up a beautiful, awe-inspiring week at San Antón for the week of 24 July to 1 August 2015. Are we home yet?

PART IV

AFTER THE WAY

'Sometimes we have to get into the storm of life and place one foot in front of the other and move in the direction we want to go.' – Angela Barnard

The Fifteenth Letter, Which I Never Sent

From: Angela Barnard,
angela@inspireforlifecoaching.com
To: Dear Friends
Subject: What was in it for me?
Date: Thursday, 17 September 2015, 17:01

Months have passed since we returned home from San Antón and Spain. While I was there, I wrote about my experiences and the lessons I was learning from being on the Camino. I pacified the concerns I had before I departed, and each day I remembered life-truths that are important to me through inspired action.

Did I find the Camino magical, as I had the year before? Yes!

Was it the Camino that was magical, or was it me? I think it was a mixture of both.

As previously, I opened myself to possibilities. Therefore, every day I experienced marvellous, unexpected blessings. What I know for sure is that when you live with expectancy you experience more inspiration. This is the challenge of my daily life: to live expecting inspiration and to allow it to flow to me, while taking action.

So why did I actually go to Spain? What was in it for me? I asked this question myself on the Thursday evening before I went to bed on my second to last night in San Antón. I never experienced a full house at San Antón. Either the mass of pilgrims would pass early in the morning, streaming from neighbouring villages, or most pilgrims would arrive in the late morning, and this was too early to stop for the day.

Each day, I would go out onto the road with oranges and ready conversation to see who might be interested in staying. Thursday was different. I had been wondering what it would be like to experience a full house, and, without me fully realising it, we were suddenly over capacity. Instead of having twelve pilgrims, we had fourteen. The thirteenth was Solomon the Donkey, and the fourteenth Rimbo, his canine companion.

What an eclectic group of people and animals! Oliver was in his element because four of the pilgrims were friends of his. It was his last night to serve at San Antón after a long month there, and it was a perfect blessing for him. One pilgrim caught my attention, and I felt instantly drawn to him. His name was Hubert, and he was a seasoned pilgrim who had walked the Camino countless times. He was walking with a friend and his twelve-year-old daughter, who has walked eight times, and his eight-year-old daughter, who has walked four times. Hubert was a gifted storyteller with immense faith and character. If you judge a person by their appearance, most people would avoid him as he appears scruffy and unkempt, but his soul is like a beacon.

The pilgrims shared stories and deep soul connections around the dinner table, and it was a wonderful evening. I decided to retire earlier than most, and, as I lay in bed, I asked myself, 'So what have you come here for? What were you supposed to hear or learn this week?' My mind immediately went to my business. I started feeling anxious, and I sternly told myself, 'Shut up Angela and sleep! This is not the time to start worrying about things.' I shut my eyes, turned over and fell instantly into a sound asleep.

During the week, we experienced a glorious full moon. As the sun set and darkness spread, the moon would rise and make an appearance through the massive windowless arch which is a focal point in San Antón. With the clear skies, full moon and the stillness of night, I felt transported to a place of tranquillity and respite each evening.

I awoke from my sound sleep at 3:10 a.m. on Friday morning and went outside to gaze at the moon. In the moonlit brightness, San Antón had an eerie stillness to it. There was no breeze blowing, no bats flying or pigeons cooing. The night was still. Gazing at the moon, it felt like I was gazing directly into a high-powered spotlight, but I held the moon's gaze. A still voice spoke to my heart. 'Angie,' it said, 'In the morning, ask Hubert for the message he has for you.'

I thought, *What the fuck?! Ask Hubert for the message he has for me? Are you fucking mad? Stop hearing strange things and go back to bed!* This is what I promptly did, and when I awoke at 6 a.m. to prepare breakfast, I wondered if I had dreamt it all. As the pilgrims came in for breakfast, I felt instantly drawn to Hubert once more, and I wanted to rush at him and blurt out my request. However, I powerfully resisted. Eventually, I could not take it any longer. I felt compelled to relay the message to him, so I followed him outside when he went for a smoke.

I told him what I had heard, and he became very still and peered into my eyes. In his melodious French accent, he replied, 'Maybe. I will listen.'

Well, OK then, I thought. He doesn't have anything to say. I've lifted my burden; let me get on with breakfast.

After a while, Hubert sought me out and told me that he had a story to share with me. We made our way outside, and Hubert began his tale.

It was his first Camino. He felt called to walk The Way but realised that he did not have sufficient resources to leave his wife and baby at home with enough provisions and to support himself while he was on pilgrimage. He decided to walk out of his front door in France and make his way to Santiago de Compostela. Deep within his spirit he knew that he should go with nothing but the few clothes that he had, with no money for food or accommodation, and that he should ask for help as he went. He left home with a reasonably sized baguette, some water and a kilogram of salt.

The weather was very hot, and, within the first day, he had consumed his bread and water. (Who knows what happened to the salt.) The next morning, he was walking past a farmhouse. The kitchen window flew open, and an old man called to him. 'Hey guy! Where are you going?' he asked. Hubert explained that he was on his way to Santiago de Compostela. 'Wait a moment. I have something for you,' the old man called, and through the window he handed Hubert a day-old piece of baguette. Hubert was grateful for this gift and continued on his way.

By the third day, he was becoming concerned. He had only had these few morsels of bread to eat, the weather was extreme, and there seemed no end to his suffering in sight. Along the way, he passed a woman. 'Hey guy!' she said, 'Where are you going?' Yet again, Hubert explained his mission, and she gave him a dry, hard piece of baguette, approximately fifteen centimetres long.

By the fifth day, he felt like he could no longer continue. Doubts, insecurities, fears, hunger and exhaustion overwhelmed him. He was convinced that he should return home as his God had abandoned him and there was no help for him along The Way, only certain starvation and suffering. Once again, an old man asked him where he was going, and in response to his answers bestowed a tiny piece of rock-hard, week-old bread upon Hubert.

This was the last straw. Weary to the point of delirium he collapsed on the side of the road to have a rest. Overwhelmed with emotion, he cried and felt desolate and abandoned by God and man alike. After a while, he became aware of a shadow falling upon his back, and he turned to see who was behind him. There was no person there but rather a statue of the Virgin Mary was giving him respite from the blazing sun. In the stillness of his heart, he felt that he should open his bible and read a random scripture. He obeyed, and what he read was this: 'Are not five sparrows sold for two pennies? Yet not one of them is forgotten by God. Indeed, the very hairs of your head are all numbered. Don't be afraid; you are worth more than many sparrows.'

I was fully engaged in Hubert's story, as I am sure you are, but as I heard this, I dissolved into 'ugly-cry mode'. Actually, it was not crying. I wept! As clearly as I have a nose on my face, I knew that was why the Camino recalled me: to be clearly, powerfully, emphatically reminded of the truth that I need to hold onto and never let go of.

While I am not a practising Christian, I know and experience Spirit daily in my life. Once again, Spirit was lovingly reminding me, 'You have purpose. You have value. Fear not, all is well.'

As I inelegantly wiped tears and snot from my face and tried to control my weeping-induced hiccups, Hubert continued with his tale. As the message from his bible and the cool shade created by his stone companion sank into his heart, he knew, without a shadow of a doubt, that all would be well. He sat and cried with joy and gratitude, allowing peace to nurture and console him. He did not seek to hide away in shame as he sat crying on the side of the road but rather simply allowed the lesson to find its space within his heart.

A short while later, a man stopped next to him in a van. 'Hey guy,' he said, 'is everything OK?'

'Yeah, yeah,' Hubert assured the friendly stranger. 'All is well.'

'Why don't you join me?' the man asked. 'I am driving to the next town, which is 4 kilometres away. Perhaps you are going in the same direction and could use the ride.'

Hubert immediately faced a dilemma. Was the man sent to distract him from The Way? Was he a wolf in sheep's clothing or the Devil in disguise trying to lead him astray? After a brief internal battle with himself, he decided to accept the friendly stranger's offer and drive with him to the next town.

As he threw his bag into the back of the truck, he felt a clear message come to his spirit. 'Hubert,' it said, 'from now on you must not tell people where you are going or what you are doing. You must not ask for food or accommodation.' Wow! What a tall order. Was this insane or what? Yet he felt the absolute truth of this instruction, and took it to heart. As he drove to the next village with his companion, he felt like a naughty little boy who is holding a precious secret but can't let the cat out of the bag. He spoke exuberantly about everything else but studiously avoided the obvious topic: where he was going and what he was doing.

In the next village, he disembarked from the van, wished the driver a friendly adieu and went on his way. Moments after finding the Camino and beginning his walk again, the driver of the van came running after him. 'Hey guy! Wait! Don't go! I have something for you!' The man handed Hubert a large bag. Viewing the contents, he was shocked. The man explained to him that he was a supervisor of a four-man road crew, and the bag contained all their food for the day. Enough to feed five labouring men! Hubert did not want to take the bag, but his companion insisted: 'No! No! You must! You need this, and you must take it.' From that moment until he reached Finisterre, weeks later, he never once asked for food or shelter. It was simply provided for him by angels along The Way.

As he concluded his tale, and I attempted to collect myself, I explained to him the reason for my profuse tears. 'You see, it is so!' he said.

Do you know that feeling within yourself when truth or enlightenment lands within your body? It looks for a place to settle, to balance, to breathe, to spread and to fill the empty spaces. It does not seek to conquer or destroy, it simply wants to transplant all doubt, banish all resistance and obliterate all fears. It feels heavy and yet it is so light. It is dense with absolute love and pure knowledge, and it gently spreads throughout the body, lands within the heart and mind and fills the soul, and you know – absolutely *know* – that you have received directly from the source of All Knowing, The One. This was my exact experience.

As the pilgrims departed, and I cleaned San Antón and prepared to fetch The German from Sahagún, I allowed the joy of deep knowing to settle fully within my body. While I certainly had not forgotten the powerful lessons I had learnt the year before, this felt different, like a deep inner settling, truth pushing out doubt, taking up residency, becoming imperial within me. I felt the temptation to be overawed by this message, to become slightly numb. Instead, I allowed the joy of deep knowing to cradle me in its loving care.

I met The German and, over *café con leche*, told her what had occurred. We both cried together, comprehending that the simple congruency with which Spirit had spoken to me was not serendipitous. Returning to San Antón, we went via Moratinos to see Rebekah. It was a lovely visit, filled with fellowship and love. As we made our way to the front door, Rebekah said to me, 'Angie, you really need to start living who you are. You are really coming into your name, you are an angelic messenger; this is who you are and must be.'

Could the day become any stranger? Could the message be any more powerful? Rebekah, to whom I had spoken once over Skype, a few weeks previously, and who I had met briefly at San Antón, was now my oracle. I did not dissolve into ugly-cry mode once again but comprehended that truth bombs were been thrown my way, and I knew that I had to remain vigilant.

As she kissed me farewell, she left me with this beautiful quote from Macrina Wiederkehr: 'I will believe the truth about myself no matter how beautiful it is.' How often do we fall into believing that the truth about ourselves is horrible or holds deep, dark secrets, and yet each of us come from love, we are returning to love. The beauty within is astounding. It is while accepting and believing in this beauty that we stumble around in the dark.

As I write this, I once again marvel at the journey of my life. It fills me with delight, and I feel immense joy to have this wonderful experience we all call life to continue creating the beautiful masterpiece of my unfolding soul.

What does it mean to be an angelic messenger? I mean, seriously, are you really asking me this?! What do I know?! I am still figuring this out! What I am learning is that each day I must wake up and be present to this life, *compos mentis*, that I must not fall asleep or become distracted with irrelevant trivia. Finding my 'voice' has often left me feeling doubtful, but it's in those moments that I now know to be bold and to press on regardless of my fear and confusion.

I walked 900 kilometres across Spain to be able to say I walked into me, I came home to myself, I found the seat of my soul.

Or did I?

The Sixteenth Letter from Holzminden, Germany

From: Angela Barnard,
angela@inspireforlifecoaching.com
To: Dear Friends
Subject: Losing the illusion
Date: Thursday, 19 October 2017, 00:45

It was Wednesday, 20 January 2016. Snow had fallen overnight, and a beautiful winter wonderland greeted me as I looked out the door. I felt a strange compulsion to walk. I wanted to accomplish two things: to walk to the railway lines at the bottom of my road and make a small video to post on Facebook later; and then to walk to 'clear my head'. You see, two things were weighing on my mind. One was a sense of deep gratitude for how far I had come, and the other was a great sense of being stuck. Talk about an oxymoron!

I put on my winter woollies and left the house. I planned to have a shower when I returned as I had three appointments set up later in the morning. At the railway tracks, I made my video, speaking about the sense of freedom I felt in my life and the great gratitude I felt to be alive. You've read about the work situation that left me battered and broken, but I haven't told you that there were times when I believed that standing in front of a train was a viable solution to end my misery. The despair I felt was debilitating, and this was one of the darkest periods of my life.

While I never believed in a million years that anything in life could cause me to sink into such despair, there I was, feeling like this was a viable resolution to my pain. What made it worse was this inability to access myself, to pull myself out of despair and fight back. This, of course, was an illusion appearing real. It wasn't until anger sparked within the consuming numbness that I began the journey back to myself, and you've read how the Camino was a massive part of my journey. Yet here I was, six months after returning from San Antón, feeling stuck within my business and myself yet again. You know all of us have an Achilles heel, and this appears to be mine: getting stuck – or, better yet, believing that I am stuck. You may even be thinking, *What the fuck is the matter with this woman!?* I don't blame you, I sometimes think that myself.

Returning to that snow-covered morning, I found myself wanting to run or, rather, to walk away. As I passed through the fields, I walked up a slight incline and felt a deep longing within myself to escape my situation. While I had returned from Spain full of clarity and inspiration, I had made a fatal mistake. I forgot to remember. I forgot to hold dear. I forgot to live my truth. Instead, I was caught up in the busyness of trying to create a business, to make it happen. Frankly, I lost my way. Seriously? How fucking boring is this?! The same behaviour pattern repeatedly: Angela not trusting in herself and her message.

As I was having these hateful inner dialogues with myself, I paused for a moment and turned around to admire the landscape. I remembered how I often did that on the Camino. After walking a while, I would pause, turn around and admire the landscape I had just walked through. As I did this on that Wednesday morning, I felt a deep longing for the Camino. A deep longing for the connectedness, the freedom, the clarity, the simplicity. Perhaps a deep longing for my best self. As I conversed with myself and battled to overcome the propensity to leave, I said to myself, 'Angela, you put on your big-girl panties, and you finish what you've started. There is no running away!' I admired the view one last time and continued up the slight incline.

I had walked less than 100 metres around a bend when I heard a loud cracking sound like a branch falling and breaking. Then I realised I was lying in the snow in agony. That 'loud branch breaking' wasn't a tree – it was some part of my body. While I could see no evidence of ice where I had fallen, I had lost my footing and broken a bone. The pain was excruciating, and I was alone in a field, with a low phone battery and limited options.

I knew I couldn't call an ambulance. How the hell was I going to tell them where I was, in German! I could barely think straight in English, let alone attempt to give an emergency operator directions to my location in a foreign language. I called The German, and, in between heaving breaths, told her I had broken something and needed help. The problem was that she couldn't reach me by car, and I had to make my way to the nearest road, which was 400 metres up a hill.

I made my way slowly up the hill, crossing the railway line and praying a train wouldn't come chugging along. Stumbling uphill, I felt something within me shift. I started to weep. It was a deep mourning weep, and it felt less about physical pain and more about releasing an emotional or spiritual burden. I knew that whenever 'this' situation was over, it would be set differently than how it was before, and as I stumbled and crawled, I wept knowing that was how it was meant to be.

I was blessed to find a barrier at the roadside that I could rest upon as I waited for The German to find me. That road is infrequently used by the military and farmers and leads to a military training facility in the forest. As I sat on the barrier, I heard a loud noise that sounded like a truck coming down the hill at high speed. I could not see the vehicle because it was in a curve, but, from the sound of it, I thought it was rather large and travelling too fast. My monkey mind kicked in, and I imagined a gigantic vehicle careening downhill and losing control in the icy conditions. Taking speed, angles and curves into account, I calculated that I was bound to die a miserable and violent death when the truck smashed into the barrier.

What could I do? It wasn't as if I could hightail it to the other side of the road to avoid impending death, so instead I braced myself on the barrier and prepared to meet my maker. When the vehicle came into sight, it wasn't a truck but rather a snowplough clearing the road. The driver never reduced speed but came around the bend with the plough down, and, at the given speed, the plough at a perfect 45-degree angle, it dumped metres of snow directly onto my freezing ass. My response was to promptly burst out crying.

This wasn't weeping. Oh, no, this was full-on self-pitying wailing. There I was, on the barrier, barely able to stand, completely covered in wet, heavy snow. I stood and tried to shake myself like a wet dog, all the while wailing in self-pity and feeling completely miserable that The German hadn't arrived quickly. When she did arrive, she jumped out of the car to help me. She had a coke in one hand and a chocolate in the other, and, when she saw me she exclaimed, 'Oh Bella! You're as white as snow!' I mean really! How rude!

At the hospital, I discovered that I had broken my ankle in two places. I was fortunate not to require surgery, but would wear an Air Cast for six weeks. This was the first time I'd broken a bone, and, to be honest, it was a relatively painless experience. The German would massage my leg and foot each night, and this aided the healing process immensely. The whole experience required a complete readjustment, and I remained relatively calm and unmoved throughout. I didn't allow myself to become caught up in the drama but realised that I had created a physical manifestation of what I had been feeling emotionally and spiritually. I had created more immobility and stuckness for myself.

The 'healing' process proceeded as expected, and even dealing with an unfriendly one-legged doctor didn't faze me too much. I worried that when the Air Cast was removed I wouldn't be able to walk properly, but with physiotherapy I was able to start being independent again. However, after a few weeks, I realised that 'something' was wrong. While the X-rays showed that my foot had healed, I was experiencing incredible pain. How could this be? After experiencing little or no pain during the six-week healing period, I was now riddled with pain. I found it difficult to walk, and my bones just didn't feel right. Six months after my fall I had another MRI and was informed by the radiologist that my foot was still broken. How could this be? Another six weeks later, after consulting an orthopaedic surgeon, I was told, 'There's nothing wrong with your foot, you're healed.' In this confusion, and regardless of what the experts were telling me, my foot felt neither whole nor healed.

By September, I had simply had enough. The pain, the immobility, the uncertainty … I was done with all that shit. I awoke one morning and decided: 'This is it! Be healed!' After making such a clear, resolute decision, I started to gain positive mobility in my foot. The pain receded, and I began to feel like I could get on with my life. Actually, I think I was simply perpetuating my own stuckness. I was physically manifesting a situation that I was feeling within. For months, I had been feeling like something was seriously wrong in my business. I wasn't getting the results I was working so hard to achieve. Something seemed off. I had followed all the formulas. I had implemented all the strategies. I was doing all the things the experts said to do, and yet it felt totally misaligned and like I was going nowhere fast. In terms of 'running a business', I was doing everything right, and yet it didn't feel that way.

By the end of October, I couldn't take it any longer. I was no longer willing to continue doing what I was doing and feeling so crap about it. I decided to have a day of silence, created a woman cave in my office and vowed not to come out until I knew what was wrong and how to fix it. It was in silence that the answers came to me. When you walk the Camino, the number-one thing every pilgrim must do is look for the yellow arrows. If you don't look for the arrows (which can be found literally everywhere along the path), you will get lost. It's as simple as that.

I decided to look for the arrows within my business and my life. What had I seen but not taken notice of? What had I overlooked? It became clear to me that throughout the year I'd been hearing the same thing from different sources, either from conversations with people, what I'd read, news from friends and colleagues. The buzzwords were 'Akashic Records', 'soul' and 'alignment'. The Akashic Records are an energetic database, located in the spiritual realm, that contain a record of every choice ever made. Each soul has its own Akashic Record that contains all the information about the soul back to the moment of creation by Spirit. Some of this sounded like gobbledygook when I first heard it, but I also noticed that I had been wantonly obtuse at times when presented with a new way of thinking. My day of silence also showed me clearly that I wasn't expressing a very important part of myself in my business, namely the core of my being. I wasn't being an angelic messenger.

So what happened? Well, as tends to happen, when I start in a certain direction, guess what? The Universe conspired to show me the way. As I started asking questions about the Akashic Records and who I am at soul level, different trainings presented themselves to me, all centred around this topic. I found myself veering off at a 90-degree angle, learning new skills, discovering new parts of myself, stepping into new levels of consciousness.

When it comes to exercising my angelic-messenger superpower, I am still not doing this fully. While I help others step into themselves, I find myself in a state of resistance, not always willing to step fully into my own divine power. Some days I seriously wonder why I sabotage myself, why I make things so difficult, why I simply don't remain in the present, follow joy as my guiding emotion and keep things simple. Why would I do that? Why would I make my life easier, when I seem to have mastered difficult?! Yet, as with everything in life, every journey starts with a single step. Therefore, if I want different, then I have to take a step in that direction and take different actions to affect change in my life.

In the past year, I have come to realise so many things both about myself and about this thing called life. One of my earliest memories is of me as a child of seven years old asking, 'Is this it? Is this what life is? Surely there is more to life than this?' From this young age, I doubted that 'this was it', I always felt that life had to have some bigger meaning, some greater purpose. Now I know with certainty that life is meaningless and then we die. Yes, you read that correctly: life is meaningless, and then we die. No, I'm not pissing on your parade and being negative. The fact that life is meaningless and then we die is one of the most life-affirming positive realisations you can come to.

This is why I say so. From the youngest age, I followed the doctrine of Christianity. I sought God's purpose for my life and to do His will. I tried my best to love God and be His humble servant. I tried to follow His commandments and live according to His purpose for my life. I had a relationship with 'my saviour' and did my best to ensure that when I died I would fly and not fry. I looked for God without, meaning outside of myself, striving to know Him without fully understanding the God within.

I observe so many people follow a God that humankind has created in its own image rather than in God's image. As humans, we only know in part. While we come from the limitless infinite, we are so conditioned in our thinking that we can barely comprehend what it means to have the same divine power that holds the Sun in the sky and revolves the Moon around the Earth within us. We seek to be 'spiritual' without actually realising that this is exactly who we are. We are spiritual beings having a physical experience. We are God made manifest as flesh.

If I want my life to have meaning and purpose, I must create it. I don't need to look to God for permission or direction. I need to look within. I need to constantly ask myself: What purpose do I want to have in life? How meaningful do I want my life to be? What kind of impact would I like to leave on my environment? How much joy can I experience each day? Life is a series of small and large choices, and with that comes great responsibility.

In my opinion, this is where we are failing in society. Humankind is abdicating responsibility for its choices and therefore we are not living empowered or inspired lives. We seem to be more than happy to assume responsibility for the good things we create, but when life doesn't pan out as planned, then we often look for a scapegoat. This behaviour is utter bullshit. None of us can fully own our divine power without taking full responsibility for all our choices and their consequences. I feel like I am on a soapbox, yelling this message out into the world, which is not my intention. As you can see, I feel passionately about this because I see how choice is the foundation to everything. How we choose is quite literally how we live.

I believe that when I am feeling stuck, I am making this choice for myself. Life is about motion, namely forward motion. Our lives progress through various cycles, and, although we may be standing still on some level, we are always moving forward, if only towards our own departure. The most powerful tool any of us can use on a daily basis is the power of choice, preferably making life-affirming choices.

The reality is I am not stuck and have never been stuck in my life. What I do and have done is make choices that reaffirm my story of being stuck. There is no physical, mental, emotional or spiritual element within me that is at any moment stuck. This is my own illusion and one that I often recreate for myself. Now you may be thinking, 'Oh that poor miserable woman, what a silly tart she is!' and you're right, but let me just say, 'Darling, look for your own illusion. What is your Achilles heel? What is that one thing – or perhaps many things – in your life that regularly appear and knock you upside of your head?'

The fact is that life is hard. Anyone who tells you otherwise is full of shit, but, as I learnt on the Camino, 'Pain is inevitable, but suffering optional.' It is always a choice. Be encouraged to use the power of your choice to release your illusions and step more into the fullness of who you really are. For me, this past year has been about a deeper connection to myself at soul level, really understanding my soul blueprint and aligning more fully with it. Have I mastered this yet? Hell, no! However, I am moving in the right direction. I am making choices that are helping me to align more quickly when I go off track. The challenge is to recognise when I'm off track and to bring myself back to myself as quickly as possible. For me, it's all about not creating the illusion of being stuck but continuing to look for and follow the yellow arrows.

The Seventeenth Letter from Holzminden, Germany

From: Angela Barnard,
angela@inspireforlifecoaching.com
To: Dear Friends
Subject: Don't fear walking into the storm
Date: Friday, 24 November 2017, 07:36

It was the week before I was due to depart for Spain, and I was having terrible nightmares. I dreamt of being caught in the most dreadful storms, of finding no shelter and having to sleep outside. Of horrible *hospitaleros* and people doing me bodily harm. I would wake up shaking, sweating and feeling overwhelmed by fear. In my dreams, I was walking a walk that I dreaded in reality.

As I had not done enough training in preparation, one morning I decided to walk to The German's parents' house. They live 13 kilometres from us, and I thought a round trip would do my legs good. My walk took me through the neighbouring village and adjacent farmlands. As I walked, I encountered a bunny rabbit.

This surprised me as I very seldom see animals as I walk. The rabbit popped onto the pathway in front of me and sat there munching food. After a moment observing me, it went on its way.

I proceeded for another half a kilometre but started having the feeling that I needed to return home. No! This could not be! I was not going to abandon my walk, I had to complete it. I had to get the kilometres into my legs. I had to persist and not give up. I had to remember that on the Camino I wouldn't be able to just stop and go home. However, the feeling intensified, and I found myself in a right royal battle with my monkey mind.

I was approaching another small hamlet called Forst, which was the halfway mark, and the feeling to return home had not passed. Suddenly, another bunny rabbit popped onto the pathway in front of me. *What's with all the bunny rabbits?* I wondered. No sooner had I thought this, when I heard the little bunny rabbit beckon me: 'Come on, come on,' it called, 'follow me, this is the way, this is the way.'

As crazy as it sounds, my resistance to continuing on the path was extreme. I had the feeling that while the bunny rabbit was beckoning me in the direction I needed to walk, to follow it would be a huge mistake. Yet there I was, conflicted, knowing that I needed to complete what I had started but feeling that I needed to change my plan. After quite a few moments dilly-dallying in uncertainty upon the path, I decided that I wouldn't walk the way I had just come but would, rather, walk along the river to return home.

When I turned around, I nearly shat myself! Hanging over my hometown were the blackest, densest storm clouds I have ever seen. They made the storms in my dreams seem like a Disney movie in comparison. My immediate reaction was to want to turn back around and flee in the direction of Forst, but, 'No!' my spirit was telling me, 'Walk! You need to return home.' To say that I was scared is an understatement. The storm that was brewing was going to be a humdinger, and I was now walking straight into it.

I watched it approach, and, at the exact moment when I reached a fork in the path, hard, stinging droplets began to pelt down. The path led to a little rest hut, and I broke into a half-walk, half-run to reach it. Sliding into the hut like Tom Cruise in *Risky Business*, my relief was short-lived because I realised that it already had an occupant. A quick glimpse made me realise that the other occupant had been living in the hut, and, on closer inspection, I realised that it was a homeless man. *Oh fuck! Now what?*

Of course, every prejudice and fear I might have held about homeless men rose to the surface, and I meekly placed myself by the exit and said, 'Hello.' I noticed that he had a bicycle with him. The German is an avid cyclist, and I have learnt a thing or two about bikes and their associated equipment. The man's equipment was in relatively good condition and the quality was of a high standard.

The rain was now falling harder, and I didn't want to be in an awkward situation with a stranger for God knows how long, so I engaged the man in conversation. I started talking to him about his bike and his life. He told me that he had been homeless for seven years and had been travelling around Germany that whole time. One morning, he awoke and realised that he was utterly miserable in his life. He had all the trappings of wealth and success, but inside he was dying. He had a successful roofing business in Bremen, a few employees, a nice house, a nice car, but everything was meaningless to him. He decided to sell everything, to present his children with their inheritance and to begin a life on the road.

When he informed his daughters of his decision, they were enraged. How could he be so foolhardy and irresponsible? How could he throw away all he had worked so hard for to assume a life of a vagrant? They refused their inheritance and cut all ties with him, so he placed the money in trust funds, bought a bicycle and other necessary equipment and cycled away from his life as he knew it.

I asked him how he supported himself. Did he keep any of the money to be able to live? Did he miss the creature comforts and the life he once knew? He told me that he did not keep any of the money and explained that as an officially registered homeless person he could go to the unemployment office each day and receive €7 from the State. He found this to be more than enough to cover his needs. When he needed more money for repairs to his equipment he took on piecemeal jobs, and the money lasted him quite a while. He had a tent, which he used in emergencies, but he loved most of all to sleep outdoors. I wondered how he managed in winter, as winters can be extreme in Germany, and he told me that it was one of his favourite times. In recent years, his daughters had made peace with his decision, and he had spent Christmas with his children in Bremen. He did say that when he stayed with them he felt like he had cabin fever and wanted to be outdoors once again.

A few things struck me immediately about this man. He was incredibly well spoken and well informed about world events. While he appeared homeless – he was a little raggedy around the edges – he was in no way lost, and he seemed perfectly at home within himself. He told me that the first two years of living a homeless life had been fraught with anxiety and terror. He felt in a constant state of struggle and suffering. It wasn't until he learnt to let go of attachment, especially the attachments of his mind, that he began a journey of self-discovery to find inner peace.

This man radiated peace. Every pore of his body exuded peace. He had a quiet self-assurance about himself that let me know there was nothing I could take away from him or give to him that would change him in any way. He had found himself.

I told him about the journey I was about to embark upon and how I was being tormented with nightmares. I told him of my aspirations and of the goal I had set. I shared with him how I was beset by doubts and fears although I felt extremely excited about the upcoming adventure. He listened to me with a complete stillness and then began to counsel me. He brought my attention to the storm raging around us and reminded me that everything rises and then passes, and that, regardless of the outcome, or my interpretation of the outcome, that all would be well.

He shared so many of his own experiences with me regarding facing fears and walking – cycling, in his case – into the unknown. I became aware that I had spent over two hours with him in the hut, the storm raging around us all the while. Lightning was striking the earth and the nearby river, and we watched as streams appeared on the path.

Then he told me to put on my poncho, take my walking sticks and continue on my way. I argued with him, saying that the storm was still raging, that it was unsafe, that I would get wet, but he was quite insistent. He told me that there would always be storms in life I needed to face. My avoidance of them would not change the fact that I would have to face them. He reminded me that in life we sometimes get wet, and, you know what? That's OK! Regarding my concerns for my safety, he asked me what there was to fear. He said that lightning could strike me as I walked, or strike the hut. Either way, if I were to die on that day, all would be well. He reminded me that there was nothing to fear but fear itself.

I donned my red riding-hood poncho, picked up my walking sticks, left him in the hut and continued towards home. As I walked in the driving rain I was singing and laughing and marvelling at the incredible encounter. It was as if I had spent two hours at the feet of the Buddha, and I felt imbued with great wisdom and peace.

I have often thought about that man and that day. I feel a sense of gratitude that I did not complete my intended journey, that I overcame my fears and listened to my spirit. I am grateful that he kicked me out into that storm, that he reminded me of the truth that regardless of the circumstance, I – within my inner being – am always well.

There are days when I don't want to take on the storms of life, when I don't want to listen to my intuition, when I don't want to make powerful choices. Some days I forget that I am an angelic messenger, here to help myself and others find their way back to themselves. Some days I forget to create meaning and purpose and live with joy. But most days I am brave, I do listen, I do choose. Most days I do remember who I really am, I do create meaning, live with purpose and find joy. It is on these days that I am the master of my fate and the captain of my soul.

May you too be the master of your fate and the captain of your soul.

Much love. Buen Camino!

Angie

Invictus

By William Ernest Henley

Out of the night that covers me,
Black as the pit from pole to pole,
I thank whatever gods may be
For my unconquerable soul.

In the fell clutch of circumstance
I have not winced nor cried aloud.
Under the bludgeonings of chance
My head is bloody, but unbowed.

Beyond this place of wrath and tears
Looms but the Horror of the shade,
And yet the menace of the years
Finds and shall find me unafraid.

It matters not how strait the gate,
How charged with punishments the scroll,
I am the master of my fate,
I am the captain of my soul.

ABOUT THE AUTHOR

Angela Barnard's philosophy about life is, 'It's your life, LIVE IT!' She loves the unexpected and is most comfortable when she doesn't have her life perfectly planned and mapped out. This adventurous spirit has led her to live on four continents and to follow the yearning of her soul and embark unexpectedly upon the Camino de Santiago Pilgrimage. Not bound by convention, she has worked as a shoe sales person, a motorbike courier, au pair, cashier, food technologist and flavourist.

Angela was born and educated in Durban, South Africa, and today lives in Germany. She owns and operates Inspire for Life Coaching and is a coach, author and speaker. Through her life and work she inspires and motivates herself and others to know, speak, and live their truth. People who know and meet her find her very inspirational.

You can contact or follow Angela at:
Email: angela@inspireforlifecoaching.com
Website: www.inspireforlifecoaching.com
Facebook: www.facebook.com/inspireforlifecoaching
LinkedIn:
www.linkedin.com/in/inspireforlifecoaching
Twitter: @angiembarnard

Printed in Poland
by Amazon Fulfillment
Poland Sp. z o.o., Wrocław

54222222R00110